Home
Cell Groups
and
House
Churches

Home Cell Groups
and
House Churches

C. Kirk Hadaway·Francis M. DuBose
Stuart A. Wright

BROADMAN PRESS
Nashville, Tennessee

Library of Congress Cataloging-in-Publication Data

Hadaway, C. Kirk.
Home cell groups and house churches.

1. House churches. I. Wright, Stuart A.
II. DuBose, Francis M. III. Title.
BV601.85.H33 1987   253.7′6   86-23209
ISBN 0-8054-6944-3

Contents

Preface

The urban church is faced with a paradox. Literally thousands of people live in close proximity, yet the peculiar nature of urban life has apparently increased the resistance of a large share of this population to the gospel, or at least to our presentation of the gospel. The people are there but they will not attend, even in cities where the large majority of the population professes to be Christian.

In the West the problem is twofold: (1) how to activate the large pool of nominal or lapsed Christians, and (2) how to reach into the smaller but increasing population of unchurched who see no use for Christianity. In nations dominated by non-Christian religions or atheism the problem is how to begin to make an impact on a massive city where Christianity is viewed with mistrust or even hostility, and to do so with very limited resources.

In these settings our efforts have largely been confined to traditional methods. We organize the same church, with the same structure and programs, in the most diverse urban settings. In one sense, we are simply recreating what has worked for us in the past, but in another sense we may be trying to force ways of "doing church" into settings where they are inappropriate. If nothing else, we should be aware that many options already exist for ministry in the city in addition to those cherished forms which were nurtured in rural America.

As often happens, innovations in church structure have come from outside the established churches in the West. The authors, along with other observers, have detected in recent years an upsurge in activity involving home-related worship. All around us we have seen house churches, home cell groups, home fellowship groups, Bible studies, and other forms emerge and flourish in an unusual manner. Not that they are new, but the interest in such activity has increased greatly, and the forms which have emerged have done so with a greater sense of permanence than in the past. We now observe highly organized house church ministries that have every intention of remaining house churches. We see established churches all over the world adding home cell groups as a permanent part of their institutional structure. And we see home Bible studies spreading though the efforts of parachurch organizations.

The surge of interest in home-related worship has not been confined to fringe groups, even though its initial impetus was from groups outside mainline Western Protestantism. Many mainline churches have begun to experiment with home-related worship, and many more are considering the possibility. In this situation we felt that a thorough study and evaluation of home worship was needed. This book represents such an effort, and it is our hope that pastors, seminary students, planning committees, and many others will find it useful as they consider involvement in house churches, home cell groups, or one of the many other forms of Christian worship in the home.

We began our study with the purpose of conducting an objective evaluation, even though all three authors shared positive sentiments about our subject. The research increased our appreciation for the various forms of worship in the home, yet we have tried to acknowledge the negative along with the positive. We began our study with an acute awareness that we could not possibly study the entire home cell/house church movement. We chose, therefore, to include both an overview and analysis of the movement in general and several specific case studies. Better examples may well exist, and we encourage those who lead them or have studied them to make the broader Christian community aware of their presence.

The research began in early 1983 and continued into 1986. Adjustments have been made as the book progressed in reaction to changes in the groups we have studied, but the reader should be aware that changes continue in such a dynamic movement even when research and writing have ended.

Our objectives in the study should be apparent in the sequence of chapters. First, we wanted to give an overview of worship in the home as it has emerged in recent years. This overview is followed by chapters which consider church structure in its historical context and in the light of theology. In these chapters we see that the house church is more traditional than our present "traditional church," and that the Bible does not mandate any particular organizational form as the "ideal" church type. In the fourth chapter we develop a typology of groups, all of which share an emphasis on worship in the home. As a generic term we use *Christian house groups*, under which a total of five types are defined. They range from the home Bible study to the house church.

Two types of Christian house groups have created more interest and controversy than the others. They are the home cell group and the house church. Chapters 5 and 6 present case studies of each.

From case studies we move to analysis. We look conceptually at the nature and growth of Christian house group movements, the use of leadership and authority, and the problem of organizational change. The three chapters take social science approaches to these subjects. Finally, we end with a chapter which summarizes the advantages and potential disadvantages of house churches and home cell groups and which gives mainline churches and denominations options for involvement.

We hope that the end result is a positive yet objective evaluation of this phenomenon. Some may feel we were too honest and may scare people away by dwelling on the negative aspects. Others may say we were not objective enough and that we should not have recommended that churches be involved with Christian house groups. In fact, there was some disagreement among the authors on this issue. The book represents a middle ground. We are positive, but we also supply those interested in worship in the home with enough information to proceed with their eyes open, wary of the pitfalls. Perhaps this book will help innovative churches and mission agencies plan for problems which will emerge and to deal with them effectively. We encourage involvement for those open to change and who have a vision for reaching the "unreachable" for Christ.

1
The Reemergence of Worship in the Home

The church is not made of bricks and mortar but of Christians. This fact has a way of being forgotten, and we routinely refer to the buildings where the church meets as "churches." The church can exist and meet anywhere, and one of the places where it is finding a home is in the houses of individual Christians all over the world. This is a trend which affects worship among Christians in China who for many years were forbidden to build free churches, Pentecostal Christians in Korea who have organized a church of over half a million members,[1] and tradition-minded denominations in the United States whose members demand a more intensive and supportive form of "church" than they currently have.

Of course, we should realize that the only thing new in all of this is the *trend*, not the fact that Christians are meeting in homes for prayer, Bible study, sharing of needs, and worship. This is, after all, the way the church began in Jerusalem, Antioch, and Rome. And we could add that Christians have been worshiping in homes in one way or another since the time of Christ. What is new is the *revival of interest* in home-related worship.

In the United States, which has lagged behind many areas of the world in developing excitement over house churches and home cell groups, we have found that innovative churches (and even those that are not known for being innovative) are exploring some variation of the Christian house group. A movement has taken shape in this nation which may prove to be a fad or may well produce a radical change in the way Americans worship. In any event, the phenomenon must be studied, understood, and evaluated by laypersons who are concerned about the lack of depth in their churches, by pastors who are considering this form of ministry, and by denominational planners who are wondering if home worship is something their denomination should pursue or something to be avoided.

Types of Christian House Groups

House churches and home cell groups are just two types of Christian groups that meet in the home. There are many others, and, in fact, we can identify immense variation in the organization of house churches and in ways "mother churches" have structured home cell or neighborhood groups. We will try to consider the full range of house groups but will focus on the two that are making the greatest impact on the Christian community today: the home cell group and the house church.

Of the many ways Christians meet in the home for some aspect of worship or "church-related" purpose, the simplest and most nonthreatening for the mainline traditional church is the *Home Bible Study.* Studying the Bible is recognized as beneficial by all churches, and Bible study groups are typically seen as a welcome supplement to Sunday School. A few pastors may worry that Bible studies not controlled by the church are apt to drift into the "never-never land" of heresy. In fact, one pastor that was interviewed on this subject remarked, "No, I do not encourage such groups because my members get enough bad teaching in Sunday School." This was not a typical response but one which denotes the suspicion some pastors have about religious meetings not controlled by an organized church.

Home Fellowship Groups are another type that we will consider. They are not as focused as are Bible studies and are thus somewhat more suspect. The goals of prayer, accountability, sharing, mutual support, and caring are somewhat vague, and it is sometimes feared that the search for a deeper life can lead such a group off the "deep end." Some Baptists are particularly wary of groups like this because of the fear that members will begin speaking in tongues. In any event, fellowship groups that meet in homes are becoming increasingly widespread as Christians in America seek close primary relationships and support in time of need.

Home Cell Groups are versions of the home fellowship groups, but they are controlled and organized by a host church. This is the model coming out of Korea where a congregation is divided into small groups which meet in the home during the week for prayer, singing, sharing, Bible study, and other activities. Such groups are being implemented by hundreds, perhaps even thousands, of traditional churches in the United States.

Base-Satellite Units are mission-type house churches which are sponsored by a host church. Unlike the home cell group, however, these units have a large degree of autonomy. They usually meet on Sunday morning in homes, rather than with the host church, and were created because of the realization that some people are uncomfortable with the traditional church setting. This is not a typical approach, but it is an experiment which seems to be working well among a number of Southern Baptist churches in Texas, Kentucky, and a few other states.[2]

The final type of group is the *House Church.* This is a group which seeks to embody all aspects of a New Testament church in a group meeting in homes rather than in a church building.

It is not a subunit of an institutionalized church like the satellite units or the cell groups, nor does it have the limited goals of the Bible study or the home fellowship group. Members are seeking to be the church in the home setting and are not members of other churches. Groups like this are not easily visible to the public, but they are becoming more widespread in the United States. Some are single churches while others are federated with several additional house churches.

This list is by no means exhaustive. Small Christian groups which meet in the home setting do so for a large variety of reasons, and if categorization were based solely on differing goals, our list would be almost endless. Campus crusade "action groups" are essentially federated Bible studies in structure, but they add a heavy emphasis on evangelistic outreach to the goal of studying the Bible. "Intentional Christian communities" like Patchwork Central in Evansville, Indiana, combine home worship and social action yet express no desire to become a church. Instead, they draw people from many churches who share a desire to respond to the needs and powerlessness of our urban poor.

A Third World Catalyst

The beginning of any movement is hard to describe because any idea has probably lain dormant in many forms, in various places. The idea catches fire in one setting and spreads rapidly, often first igniting in those places where a similar idea already existed. This has been true with Christian house group movements. Many of the groups we have contacted began without knowledge of one another, yet there is now an awareness of being part of a worldwide movement that is spreading rapidly. The catalyst which transformed the many unconnected attempts at Christian house groups into a movement was the emergence of new forms of church in the Third World. For centuries the Third World has been the recipient of missions and has often seen forms of church organization created in the West imposed upon itself with little attempt at adaptation. The churches have the same architecture, order of worship, and even the same hymns. Several Christian groups in Japan have been so well indoctrinated in American Christianity that a building is required before they feel free to constitute a church. In the past, the flow has always been one way.

The colonialism of the "first world church" has no doubt retarded mission efforts and forestalled the development of indigenous evangelical Christian movements. Is there any wonder that our mission fields remain mission fields and have not become mission senders? This situation is changing, however. The growth of evangelical churches has been so great in Korea, all over Africa, and in certain parts of Latin America that the direction of the flow may be reversing. Innovations, new ideas, new forms of church structure, and even missionaries are now beginning to flow out of the Third World back to the United States and Western Europe.[3]

One of the new structures is the basic Christian community, and another is the megachurch—organized around one form or another of a cell group/satellite structure. The largest churches in the world were once in the United States. This is no longer true. The largest of the "superchurches" in America averages thirteen thousand in worship, and the second largest has eight thousand.[4] A few others are over five thousand, but the vast majority of churches in the United States are under five hundred in membership. The largest church in the world is now the Yoido Full Gospel Church in Seoul, Korea, which numbers at least half a million in active membership.[5] It is also true that several other churches in Seoul number in excess of fifty thousand, and churches in Brazil and Chile can be found of a similar size.[6]

Given the imaginative way that members are counted in many churches, or at least never dropped off the rolls, one may legitimately wonder if the size of such churches is real. It is, and many of these churches are continuing to grow at a rapid pace. Already, the figures published in this book are too low. How have these churches grown so large? They have done so by creating new organizational forms of the church which make growth virtually unlimited. Rather than copying the traditional structures imported from the United States or Great Britain, they have modified these in resourceful and imaginative ways and have been phenomenally successful. To a certain extent, this change was a matter of adapting a form to fit a new culture, but in another sense the result was a true innovation which has proved to be exportable.

As we see it, Third World Christians were not as tied to tradition as Christians in the United States and were thus freer to experiment with new organizational forms. The pastor who has tried anything new understands that change is difficult, especially when the form which is being altered may have hundreds of years of history behind it. To tamper with the Sunday School on Sunday morning, the order of worship, and the traditional schedule of weekly services is viewed with about as much tolerance as altering the Bible. Yet on the "mission field," these traditions of church structure had not solidified to the point where change seemed heretical. As a result, new forms began to emerge, and the churches began to grow larger than they had ever grown before.

So vast was the growth experienced by churches in Korea and Latin America that missionaries in these countries and students of church growth in the United States began to take notice. How was this growth possible? Many people wanted to know. As a consequence, the churches were studied and their pastors invited to speak all over the world. Most pastors in the United States now know that the largest church in the world is not First Baptist, Dallas, but is instead located in Seoul, Korea.

The word spread that Paul Cho's church and several other huge churches in Seoul reached their massive size through home cell groups and that the technique will work anywhere. A movement began, and pastors have flocked to Korea to learn. Everywhere we travel, pastors express a great interest in home cell groups or house churches and ask if they will work for them. Churches all over the world are beginning to adopt the home cell group as an organizational tool. At the same time, churches that were already involved in a similar form of ministry are beginning to see their efforts as part of something larger —something that may well alter the course of the church for generations to come.

In a real sense, the growth of the Yoido Full Gospel Church and the Young Nak Presbyterian Church has galvanized attention around a new idea, created a focus, and birthed a movement which is just beginning to impact mainline denominations in the United States.

An overview of the Yoido Full Gospel Church is presented by Paul Yonggi Cho in *Successful Home Cell Groups.*[7] In this book Cho discusses how the idea for home cell groups began in the mid-sixties through a study of the Book of Acts. He became aware that in the early church, worship took place in two settings: the Temple and the home. In his church and nearly all others, worship was limited to large gatherings or to the "temple" form, and there was a total neglect of worship in the homes of believers. Cho also came to the realization that

home worship groups were the only way that such large numbers of converts could have been effectively absorbed into the
early church in such a short period of time. The three-thousand
converts on the Day of Pentecost and the five thousand on the
following day were obviously too many for the apostles to teach
and serve. Their needs were met in small groups meeting in
homes, led by persons who were probably not apostles.

If the Yoido church, which numbered twenty-four hundred
at that time, could be divided in a manner similar to that of the
early church, perhaps Cho could then be freed to preach, teach,
and equip lay leaders for ministry. The task of caring for members would thus be spread out. There would be no limits to
growth because everyone would be ministered to by people they
knew personally.

The phenomenal growth which eventually occurred in the
Yoido Full Gospel Church was not immediate, nor did the
leaders of Cho's congregation immediately recognize the wisdom of his plan.[8] In fact, the situation was far from that of the
autocratic pastor forcing a docile church to do what he wished.
Instead, all of the problems that would occur if an American
church tried to institute the plan also occurred in Korea.

The leaders of the church did not accept Cho's plan. The men
said they were too tired after a long day of work to lead a home
cell group. So Cho turned to the women of the church, despite
the fact that placing women in positions of leadership violated
cultural norms in Korean society. The city was divided into
twenty districts with a woman over each district, and the plan
was announced to the congregation on the following Sunday.
Meeting locations were distributed, and the members were
asked to attend the cell group in their area.

The plan was not an instant success. Only one member in six
attended their assigned cell group, and other problems arose

with increasing regularity. Most of the problems were solved, however, when some organization was imposed on the groups. Initially, there was no real organization; group leaders did whatever they saw fit. Cho began to train the leaders, a uniform message was to be taught, the length of meetings was limited, the serving of meals was eliminated, and a maximum size was determined.

More and more cell groups came into being, their numbers increasing from twenty to 150.[9] Further, the numbers continued to grow because a growth strategy was built into each cell group. The groups were to be evangelistic and to invite new persons to join their cell. As new families were added, a person was also being trained to lead a new cell group when it came time to divide. When the group reached fifteen families, the cell divided into two groups, one led by the first leader and the other by his or her trainee. In this manner the cells grew in number in an almost exponential fashion, resulting in the largest church the world has ever seen. It now has fifty-thousand cell groups and over half-a-million members. Using similar principles the Young Nak Presbyterian Church has in excess of sixteen-thousand home cell groups.[10]

The secret of the Yoido Full Gospel Church is rather simple. It is filling a need in the lives of Christians for small-group worship and for the caring and support of friends they come to know and trust. Furthermore, it is doing all of this in a way that naturally results in evangelistic growth. It is a formula which meets universal human and spiritual needs, and as such it should fit any culture.

The principles taught by Cho have now been learned by thousands of pastors and laypersons. Churches from Korea, Japan, Australia, South America, Europe, and the United States have adopted the cell group strategy. There is a movement underway which is being championed by some and resisted by others, and it is too soon to guess whether the home cell group will become a natural part of church life in the United States, as did Sunday school in the mid 1800s, or remain a new form of church structure seen as better suited to oriental cultures.

A Parallel Movement

House churches have probably always existed, but they have not always had a common name or been visible as a movement. Now, however, the emergence of home cell groups, the proliferation of home Bible studies, and the reports of millions of Chinese in house churches has created an awareness among house churches in the Western world that they are part of something quite large. The house church movement is spreading and gaining strength in nations all over the world.

Fifty thousand or more house churches presently exist in China.[11] They are attended by millions of Chinese. No one really knows how many, but some estimates run more than twenty million.[12] In terms of sheer numbers, these figures make China the center of the house church movement.

How did this happen? Persecution made house churches necessary. As students of foreign missions know, China was the center of a large mission effort until the Communists came to power in 1949. By 1953 almost every foreign missionary was forced to leave, and the fate of the Chinese church was left in the hands of an estimated one- to two-and-a-half million Christians.[13]

Rather than outlawing Christianity from the start, the new regime in China chose to gain control of the church by consolidating all Protestant denominations and independent Christian groups into a single denomination, the Three-Self Patriotic

Movement (TSPM). According to one publication, the TSPM functioned in the 1950s as an organ of the Chinese Communist Party.[14] Its leaders, by and large, were liberal Christians who freely mixed politics with a nominally Christian message. Evangelicals were actively persecuted by the TSPM, and many churches were closed. Some two-hundred churches in Shanghai were reduced to twenty-three and over sixty in Peking to only four.[15]

With the closure of so many churches and the imposition of strict regulation of Christian activity, many Christians in China went underground and began meeting in their homes for worship. Without buildings, trained leadership, and often without Bibles, the house churches began to emerge in 1955 and slowly and quietly spread across China. The cultural revolution in the 1960s produced an even more intense wave of religious persecution. The party-controlled Three-Self Movement and all other formal expressions of religion were attacked and destroyed. All church buildings in China were closed, and for thirteen years house churches were the only organized expression of Christianity in China.[16]

During the cultural revolution, house churches survived and grew in spite of persecution. The situation seems remarkably similar to that of first-century Christians and their persecution by the Roman Empire. Worship in the home in small groups became the only safe way Christians could meet. Rather than withering away as the authorities expected, the movement grew. Similarly, in China the Christian movement grew as no one in the Western world anticipated. And at least some of the credit must be given to the form of worship that developed. Christians meeting in homes for worship among friends evidently had a quality that drew people to the gospel of Christ. Despite the risk, neighbors, friends, and family were invited to participate. Many were won, and the groups grew, divided, and continued to grow.

Since the death of Mao and with the beginning of Deng Xiaoping's push toward modernization, the pressure on religious activity has eased. The number of house churches increased dramatically as a result, with many young people becoming especially responsive to the gospel. Many, in fact, were former Red Guards who helped destroy many churches and other institutions in Chinese society.

Now, however, the house churches in China are being threatened in another way. In 1979 the Three-Self Movement was allowed to reorganize, and its leaders began to insist that house churches cease to meet. The effort to reestablish control of the church in China under the TSPM has begun anew, and a number of house church leaders have been arrested.[17] Public worship is once again legal in China, but the numbers of church buildings are too few to contain more than a small percent of the Christians (four thousand government-sponsored churches for twenty million or more Christians).[18] Yet wherever a TSPM church is reopened, intense pressure is put on the house churches to disband.

The future of Christian worship in China is still in doubt because government policy which allows open worship can easily remove the privilege. Many believers remain suspicious of the Three-Self churches, and home worship continues. Persecution still exists, but it fluctuates in its intensity.

House Groups as Protest

Wherever church activities are banned or tightly controlled, it appears house groups are becoming the vehicle through which Christians can meet and worship as they please. There is still the danger of arrests, beatings, and police raids, but the groups may appear less a threat to totalitarian regimes because they are not an *open* challenge to authority. In addition, by being less visible than even the few legalized churches, house groups do not demonstrate to foreigners the embarrasing fact that religion is refusing to wither away.

China provides the most dramatic example of how house churches may take the place of institutionalized churches which are banned or begin to be vehicles of propaganda. House churches also exist in the Soviet Union where they supplement the relatively few open churches. Here, unlike China, there has not been a heavy-handed effort to merge all Christian groups into a single state-controlled denomination. Pastors are not party members preaching socialism but instead are actual Christians who preach as they wish, assuming they do not criticize the state. They must watch what they say, but it is possible to preach a gospel message without automatically being arrested.

In the USSR, house churches provide a way for believers to worship out of the eyes of the state. They also provide space for new people that the open churches may not have. The building of new church buildings is strictly controlled by the government, and there is little effort on the part of the state to respond to a need for new church buildings. Churches are an embarrassment in the Soviet Union and are certainly not supposed to grow.

House churches are also a way Christians can meet in relative safety in nations where it is Christianity or Protestantism that is condemned rather than religion in general. Churches meet with great disapproval in Muslim nations, and it is often illegal to try to convert Muslims to Christ. Foreigners risk deportation in Saudi Arabia for holding Christian worship services, despite the fact that no efforts are made to invite Muslim citizens.

House churches may be the only way that Christians can meet and not offend their Muslim hosts.

In a similar fashion, although usually not so extreme, heavily Roman Catholic and Eastern Orthodox countries may be very antagonistic to Protestant worship. It is illegal to proselytize, for instance, in Greece, and several Protestant leaders recently received long jail terms for allegedly violating this statute. In some parts of the Philippines, Southern Baptist missionaries have come very close to being stoned by overly zealous Catholics who were instructed by their priests to have nothing to do with the Americans.[19] In such villages, house churches may be a less threatening way of beginning a mission effort until better relations can be established with the local Catholic authorities.

Another expression of the house church "as protest" that has emerged in the past twenty years is the countercultural house church. This form is largely a reaction against institutionalized churches and is most often found in Western Europe and the United States. A number of books have been written about these house churches, and it appears that this movement began in the 1950s but did not really catch fire until the late 1960s and early 1970s. This was a time of widespread social experimentation and was also marked by dissatisfaction with any and all established societal institutions.

The counterculture had emerged and with it an ideology of rejection rather than replacement. Young people, especially, felt free to experiment, and the institutionalized church was not spared its share of criticism and defection. In England, Germany, the United States, and other nations, young Christians began to withdraw from established churches and either rejected Christianity altogether or at least the overly staid, unexciting cultural religion they felt their parents exhibited. A myriad of forms emerged, some with cultic characteristics, others that simply sought a deeper, more spiritual form of Christianity.

In England, the roots of the house church movement go back to the late 1950s and are associated with the larger Charismatic movement.[20] Many of those who were converted or who simply had received "the baptism of the Spirit" began to question aspects of church structure. Often the conclusion was that denominations were wrong and that Christians needed to return to a simpler form of worship, one without the external trappings which seemed to quench the Spirit. House churches were the result in many cases.

A similar situation existed in the United States, and with the coming of the counterculture, this fledgling movement experienced a great expansion. Now, however, there are signs that the movement has slowed in some respects, but there are other signs that it has only changed forms and is becoming more organized.

The basic Christian communities in Latin America are yet another type of informal worship which is usually centered in the homes of Christians. Such groups have been largely organized by Catholic priests and exist to augment formal worship in Catholic churches rather than to oppose it. The component of protest which has found articulation in the form of liberation theology is directed at the state and at local political leaders. Though often radical in political philosophy, the groups see their efforts to combat oppression and poverty through structural change as part of their Christian duty. By meeting in homes or in fields, the groups retain a low profile and are too fluid and unstructured for the state to combat effectively.

House Churches as Mission Strategy

The house church has come to be largely identified as something formed in reaction to political repression or to stagnation in the institutionalized church. There is a place, however, where the house church is seen as quite normal and is used as a mission strategy by a well established and institutionalized denomination.

For years now the Southern Baptist Convention, as well as a number of other evangelical denominations and mission societies, has promoted the house church as the best way to start new churches on the foreign mission field. In South America, Europe, Singapore, the Philippines, all over Africa, in fact, everywhere they have activity, house churches are being started by general evangelists, teachers, even medical missionaries.

The reason for the emphasis on house churches is primarily one of finances. House churches are inexpensive. A missionary can start two, ten, twenty, or more in a single year with almost no investment of mission funds. All he or she needs to do is to find nationals willing to hold a Bible study in their homes, witness to other nationals, begin the meetings, and pray that eventually enough will be won to establish a church. Some will succeed, others will fail, but only time is lost.

The technique is being used with great effectiveness in both rural areas where land may be available for church sites and in large cities where a church building may never be feasible. In the Philippines, for instance, a Southern Baptist missionary began around twenty-five house churches in a previously unreached area.[21] He did this in the manner described above, going from city to city, preaching, knocking on doors and witnessing, and eventually locating a place to hold a Bible study. Many of the Bible studies developed into churches which still meet in homes.

The missionary's job is always to start the churches, not to pastor them. As soon as possible, a national pastor is trained or located to lead the house church. What happens then is up to the congregation. In many cases they may want to buy property and build a church building. Obviously, such churches do not remain house churches. In other cases, the acquisition of land is prohibitive, and the group will continue to meet in homes, dividing into two groups if the house church becomes too large. No deliberate effort is made to keep the group a house church, nor are they made to feel they are less a church because they do not have a building of their own.

House Churches and Home Cell Groups in the United States

Prior to the emergence of home cell groups on the American scene, house churches and Bible studies were the primary expression of worship in the home. As was the case in England, the development of house churches in the United States began with the charismatic movement in the late 1950s. Other expressions of this phenomenon had, of course, surfaced from time to time since the nation was founded, but we can trace the modern house church movement to the charismatics. Isolated expressions do not make a movement, however, and it was not until the late 1960s that the Jesus movement made house churches an important alternative form of organized worship.

The Jesus movement can be seen as both a result of and as a reaction to the broader countercultural movement in the West. The movement incorporated many of the anti-institutional values of the counterculture, but rather than rejecting Christianity along with its external expressions, the Jesus movement sought to form new, more vital expressions. It offered an attractive, expressive alternative for religious youth who saw stagnation in the mainline churches and who were influenced by countercultural values. At the same time, the movement offered a firm, meaningful ideology to those in the counterculture who had become disillusioned. Many converts to Christian belief came from those who reacted against the meaninglessness inherent in a hedonistic life-style which had no rules nor structures. Doing whatever one pleased was the ethic, but it was not an ethic which could be stably institutionalized, nor could it answer any ultimate questions about life.[22]

Informal "prayer and share" groups were a primary way youth in the Jesus movement worshiped. Some of the participants remained in the institutionalized churches and used the groups as a "spiritual supplement" while others reacted so negatively toward the mainline churches that the Jesus movement groups were their exclusive organized form of worship. It was these more alienated Christians who tended to form house churches. One group, which one of the authors studied, met in the home of a prosperous older man for singing, exhortation, and fellowship and yet resisted calling itself a church. It finally shifted its worship to Sunday morning, the symbolic step of meeting during the traditional church hour signifying that it had come to see itself as a church. At the same time it joined with twenty or so similar groups across the country and formed a denomination of sorts.

Other groups around the United States had less hesitation in rejecting traditional churches and forming their own. In cities all across the nation, communal "Christian houses" were formed where residents lived together under strict moral rules, prayed, worshiped, and aggressively evangelized street people, children, and anyone else who would listen. The large network of Shiloh houses, with headquarters in Oregon, is only one example of a form that was once quite widespread.

Since it was primarily the sons and daughters of liberal, white mainline church members who were rejecting the traditional church in favor of either the Jesus movement or the irreligious counterculture, it is not surprising that ministers in these denominations made an attempt to co-opt the movement by starting house churches of their own. This tendency seemed particularly strong in the United Methodist Church, and even the Southern Baptist Convention got into the act through its Church Extension Division at the Home Mission Board. However, it should be noted that the primary motivation behind the Southern Baptist effort was not to regain lost members but rather to use a new technique of church planting which might help evangelize an unreached segment of the population.

The effort on the part of the Methodists, Presbyterians, and others to start house churches resulted in a series of "how-to" books and several conferences. *The Base Church* (1973) by Charles M. Olsen is a good example, as is *The House Church* (1975) by Philip and Phoebe Anderson.[23] Both these books present an attractive case for the house church as an alternative —perhaps an even better form of worship than that provided by the traditional institutionalized church. *The House Church Evolving* includes materials from the House Church III conference held at Chicago Theological Seminary in 1975.[24] This book is more of an analysis of the house church than a promotion, and it is interesting that several authors in this edited volume speak as if the movement were ebbing.

> I've been involved in house churches as a form (outside institutionalized churches) for six and a half years, since 1968, and I think that form is definitely on the decline. . . . I now see the house church movement being much more in terms of process-

ing in the larger institutions; we need to talk more in terms of the local church.[25]

It may seem surprising for a movement to go unrecognized for several years and then to be written about only when it has almost run its course. The counterculture was relatively short-lived, however, as was the Jesus movement and the resulting surge in the house church as protest. Yet even though interest in these movements cooled greatly in the mid-1970s, their impact has continued. It has been shown by social scientists that countercultural values did not disappear; they simply diffused through the larger culture. In a similar fashion, persons involved in the Jesus movement either took their peculiar blend of socially conscious, nontraditional, and yet theologically conservative values back into the mainline churches, or they remained outside, trying to find some form of religious expression that "fit."

In our view, the house church movement is continuing, though at a slower pace, primarily through the development of "deeper life" groups, the "shepherding movement," and also through several quasi-Christian sects, particularly "The Way." The "deeper life" groups include the Community of Jesus in Massachusetts, the Church of the Savior in Washington, DC, and many other unconnected groups of house churches (with various forms of organization) who seek a more intensive form of religious faith than is the norm in mainline churches. Such groups are often communal or semicommunal and tend to keep a low profile. The emphasis is on spiritual growth, not on protest against the dominant church.

The shepherding movement is probably the most extensive expression of the house church in the United States, with branches in many cities across the country. It is a charismatic movement in that speaking in tongues and other "gifts of the Spirit" are emphasized, but the true distinguishing feature of the shepherding groups is the authority structure. Each person submits to the authority of a shepherd, essentially forming a pyramid with the founders at the top. The network is fairly loose, without the trappings of an organized denomination, but the process of institutionalization has led some groups to buy property and cease to be true house churches.

The shepherding movement capitalized on the many Christians who sought a more stable form of church structure but did not feel comfortable in mainline churches. Many are refugees from the Jesus movement who have never found a church home. House churches provide the spontaneity and informality of worship that many desire, and the authority structure provides the stability that keeps the groups from splintering.

Through the shepherding movement, the Evangelical Orthodox Church, and many other separate house church groups, the Jesus movement lives on, but in a more structured, institutionalized form. The elements of protest and rejection are still there, but they have been tempered by the creation of forms that ensure continuity while not conflicting with the countercultural values inherited from the Jesus movement.

It is unfortunate, but nevertheless true, that the questioning and lack of confidence in established institutions during the sixties and early seventies proved to be a boon for many religious sects such as the Children of God, ISKON, Meher Baba, the Unification Church, and others. In addition to these pseudo-Christian and non-Christian groups, there were others that remained Christ centered but felt free to reject current theology and either start from scratch with the Bible or the early church fathers in an attempt to recreate first-century worship. Many of these groups use the house church as their primary form of worship. Some, such as The Way, which calls its house churches "twig meetings," differ so drastically from the tenets of orthodox Christianity that they are routinely labeled a cult. Other groups differ only on issues that are not central to the gospel and are labeled peculiar but are not considered cultic.

At the same time the House Church movement was in its peak, other expressions of home-related worship continued in the United States. The Bible studies and fellowship groups persisted, and the notion also emerged of dividing traditional churches into various types of cell units. One of the best books which advocated this type of organization was *A New Face for the Church* (1970) by Lawrence O. Richards.[26] Richards saw the traditional forms of the church as no longer viable and in need of replacement by new forms of organization. Richards argued that each congregation (of no more than 250 adults) should be divided into a series of growth cells of five families or ten single adults each. The entire congregation would meet once a week for an extended period of worship, Bible study, and leadership training. The growth cells would also meet once a week for in-depth Bible study, sharing, prayer, and to "provide a close fellowship relationship in which gifts can be used, maximum spiritual growth achieved."[27]

Various other authors were pushing for essentially the same thing as Richards, and some churches did organize according to this cell group design; but it was not until the massive growth of the Yoido Full Gospel Church in Seoul, Korea, became known that the home cell group took off as a movement. Some confuse home cell groups and house churches with one another, and denominational leaders who have tried the house church and failed to see results are likely to see little value in either design. To many pastors, however, the home cell group is seen as something quite different from the often anti-institutional house church. To some it is a way to minister to all of their members more personally and effectively, and to others it is seen primarily as a way to achieve tremendous growth.

The churches that have implemented some form of home cell group in the United States after exposure to the Cho model are so many that we cannot list them here. And, in fact, no exhaustive list exists, although John Vaughn has recently tried to create one.[28] One of the best known churches is the Church on the Way in Van Nuys, California. A book appeared on this church in 1983, appropriately entitled *The Church on the Way*.[29] Among Southern Baptists, the nation's largest Protestant denomination, Hoffmantown Baptist in Albuquerque, New Mexico, has had the longest involvement with home cell groups. First Baptist of Atlanta, Georgia, also has a home cell group ministry organized after Cho's model. The pastors of both churches attended church growth seminars in Seoul and brought back plans to implement the cell group strategy in their own churches. In addition, Houston's Second Baptist church, a huge metropolitian congregation, hired Ralph Neighbour to introduce his design for "touch point" groups into this large church. Neighbour's design is not identical to the Seoul model but is essentially an elaborated form of the home cell group. It is naturally evangelistic and has been tested in a series of churches across the United States and overseas.

Word of Faith World Outreach Center and Church of the Rock in the Dallas, Texas, area, Willow Creek community in Chicago, Bellevue Baptist in Memphis, the Church of the Open Door in the San Francisco area, and many other churches in New England, the Midwest, and especially in California have begun this type of ministry. Interest has been so great that pastors of successful churches such as Jack Hayford of the

Church on the Way are besieged with requests for information. One associate pastor at this church, in fact, expressed irritation over this interest and suggested that many churches are looking at home cell groups as a gimmick for growth. In his view, they instead should be stressing discipleship training and spiritual growth within their congregations.

Despite these concerns, interest in home cell groups is building in the United States, and there are already signs from Africa, the Philippines, and, of course, Korea that the home cell group has been accepted as a normal part of a church's weekly worship schedule. Will the same thing happen here?

Need for Evaluation

The house church and the home cell groups are extremely interesting phenomena. For this reason alone, pastors, denominational leaders, and even the larger American public want more information. Yet there is a need for more than simple descriptions. Too many church leaders are implementing home cell groups without much prior thought, and too many others are resisting them because they fear change. We feel that a systematic evaluation is necessary which will point out the good along with the bad and indicate what mainline churches can expect if they make the decision to organize some form of home-related worship.

Already some of the good should be apparent. There is potential for numerical growth, for true Christian fellowship, for spiritual growth, and for a level of caring and mutual support unlikely to be found in the traditional church setting. We have worship, and we have teaching; but the kind of relationships that naturally develop in home worship tend to occur more by accident than by design in most traditionally structured churches.

The positive must be tempered by the negative, however. We have seen several churches try to implement home cell groups with too little planning and with unrealistic expectations. One result has been a backlash in some churches where older members have perceived the groups as threatening the Sunday school. Another legitimate concern is over the doctrinal direction that the groups may take if not controlled. Leaders with large egos and poor grounding in biblical teaching can lead groups astray in the direction of questionable doctrine, if not outright heresy.

In addition to questions concerning advantages and disadvantages of house churches and home cell groups, we will look into specific controversial aspects of home worship, such as leadership, authority, and the numerical growth potential of the groups. We will also consider why no church in the United States been able to mushroom in its growth using home cell groups in the manner of the Yoido Full Gospel Church or the Young Nak Presbyterian church in Seoul, Korea. Finally, we will present a series of alternative models for mainline church involvement in home-related worship. In doing so, our intent is not to suggest that all churches should be involved, but rather to say to those who have made the decision that certain steps need to be followed in order to avoid some of the most serious problems which may well arise. Further, such churches should recognize that there are various ways to organize the effort, each with different results and each with its share of problems. There has been a reemergence of worship in the home. It cannot be ignored, and it should be understood before we either reject it or jump on the bandwagon.

Now we will take an earnest look at the house church in its historical context. Its importance in Christian history has been overlooked, but the house church has been a useful and persistent form in every age of Christendom, playing a crucial part in periodic revivals and spiritual awakenings.

Notes

1. Reported in *Church Growth Today*, Jan. 1986, p. 1.

2. David Chancey, "The House Church," *Missions USA*, Jan.-Feb. 1983, pp. 57-58. Also see *The Indigenous Satellite Program Manual*, published by the church extension section of the Baptist General Convention of Texas.

3. See Peter Wagner, "The Greatest Church Growth Is Beyond Our Shores," *Christianity Today* (Carol Stream, Ill.: Christianity Today, Inc., 18 May 1984), p. 25.

4. Elmer Towns, John N. Vaughan, and David J. Seifert, *The Complete Book of Church Growth* (Wheaton, Ill.: Tyndale House, 1981), pp. 342-352.

5. See note #1, also see *Christianity Today*, 18 May 1984, p. 50; Peter Wagner, p. 29; and Towns, Vaughan, and Seifert, pp. 61-68.

6. Wagner, p. 28, 29; Towns, Vaughan, and Seifert, p. 51.

7. Paul Yonggi Cho, *Successful Home Cell Groups*, (Plainfield, N.J.: Logos International, 1981).

8. Ibid., p. 22.

9. Ibid., pp. 29,39.

10. *Church Growth Today*, March 1986, p. 2.

11. *Chinese Around the World* (Hong Kong: Chinese Coordination Centre of World Evangelism for Western Churches, May 1983), p. 6. Also see *Time* (Los Angeles: Time, Inc., 19 Oct. 1981).

12. This figure is based on estimates published in *Chinese Around the World*, May 1984, p. 9. The total number of Christians in China is unknown. The highest estimate is 50 million, and the lowest reasonable guess is 10 million. See Winston Crawley, *Partners Across the Pacific* (Nashville: Broadman Press, 1986), p. 115; and Martin L. Nelson, "Korean Church Growth Mission," *Korean Church Growth Explosion*, eds. Ro Bong and Martin L. Nelson (Taichung: Asia Theologican Association, 1983), p. 101.

13. *Chinese Around the World*, July 1983, p. 5. Also, Crawley, pp. 91-107.

14. *Chinese Around the World*, Feb. 1984, p. 4.

15. Ibid. Also see Crawley, p. 107.

16. Ibid.

17. Ibid., pp. 6-8.

18. Crawley, p. 114.

19. Charles Chilton, *Planting the House Church* (multilithed 1984). Available from the author.

20. Joyce V. Thurmond, *New Wineskins: A Study of the House Church Movement*, (Frankfurt: Verlag Peter Lang, 1982), p. 23.

21. Chilton, pp. 68-75.

22. Steven M. Tipton, "The Moral Logic of Alternative Religions," *Religion and America: Spiritual Life in a Secular Age*, eds. Mary Douglas and Steven Tipton (Boston: Beacon Press, 1983), pp. 79-110. Also see Steven M. Tipton, *Getting Saved from the Sixties* (Berkeley: University of California Press, 1982).

23. Charles M. Olsen, *The Base Church* (Atlanta: Forum, 1973); Philip Anderson and Phoebe Anderson, *The House Church* (Nashville: Abingdon Press, 1973).

24. *The House Church Evolving*, ed. Arthur L. Foster (Chicago: Exploration Press, 1976).

25. Quote from Erv Bode in *The House Church Evolving*, p. 30.

26. Lawrence O. Richards, *A New Face for the Church* (Grand Rapids: Zondervan, 1970).

27. Ibid., p. 30.

28. See *Church Growth Today*, Mar. 1986, p. 2.

29. Jack Hayford, *The Church on the Way* (Grand Rapids: Chosen Books-Zondervan, 1983).

2
The House Church and Church Structure in Christian History

The house church emerged in the New Testament era and continued as the most pervasive form of church structure until the time of Constantine. Church buildings then came into prominence, and house churches became a minor expression of church life. As renewal movements emerged in various periods of church history, the house church reappeared as a major structural expression of the renewed church. In the twentieth century and particularly since mid-century, the house church has reappeared as a striking phenomenon. Assuming a wide variety of manifestations, it is a worldwide phenomenon and is enjoying its greatest success since it was first eclipsed by the new structures which emerged during and after the time of Constantine.

The New Testament Era

The first definitive expression of the church in the New Testament was the house church. It was the most natural structure to develop because of two realities: the nature of the church itself and the nature of the social context in which the church emerged.

The apostolic church was first and foremost a community, a fellowship of faith. Moreover, the New Testament *koinonia* had a very strong "family" orientation. Paul called it the "household of God" (1 Tim. 3:15). The apostle was not making reference to an "estate" but to a "family"—the church was the assembled family of God.

In this regard, the New Testament church reflected a strong Old Testament rootage. The people of God in the Old Testament were referred to as "the children of Israel"—they were the children of God. Moreover, the Old Testament abounds in family-oriented metaphors which describe the people of God. The home was the center of religious instruction in the Old Testament period, a practice which was clearly carried through into the New Testament era.

This family-oriented New Testament community of faith did not exist in isolation but was influenced by its social context. The early church was an urban church. It first emerged in the great religious, commercial, cultural, and political urban centers of the first century: Jerusalem, Antioch, Ephesus, Corinth, and Rome. An urban society is characterized by two fundamental forms of communication: *mass communication* which reflects the public sphere of urban life and *personal communication* which reflects the private sphere. In all expressions of first-century church life, these two forms of communication transpired as the church became an integral part of its urban social context.

Mass communication took the form of mass evangelism in the New Testament. This is illustrated from Peter's sermon on the Day of Pentecost (Acts 2), Peter's sermon from the portico of Solomon (Acts 3), Stephen's sermon (Acts 7), Philip's mass evangelism in the city of Samaria (Acts 8), and Paul's sermon on Mars Hill (Acts 17). Moreover, mass meetings were also related to the ongoing expression of church life. The earliest

Christians worshiped in the Temple (Acts 5:42), and Paul rented the hall of Tyrannus in Ephesus (Acts 19:8-10).

The small-group meetings where personal communication took place were parallel to the mass meetings. We read of the early pattern of church life growing out of the mass evangelism at Pentecost: "Day by day, attending the temple together and breaking bread in their homes, they partook of the food with glad and generous hearts, praising God and having favor with all the people" (Acts 2:46). This pattern continued according to Acts 5:42: "And every day in the temple and at home they did not cease teaching and preaching Jesus as the Christ." In Ephesus, Paul augmented his mass evangelism and instruction (Acts 19:8-10) with personal evangelism in the homes (Acts 20:20-21).

The patterns of mass meetings varied in terms of locale: the Temple, in and around the synagogue, the marketplace, the open air, and such special public platforms as Mars Hill. However, in terms of the small-group meetings, one consistent setting seems to have prevailed—the home. The homes were the most ideal context for the fullest expression of the ongoing life of the New Testament church. When Saul was persecuting the church before his conversion, he sought after Christians in neither Temple nor synagogue, but in their homes. Acts 8:3 says: "But Saul was ravaging the church, and entering house after house, he dragged off men and women and committed them to prison."

From the beginning, homes appeared to be the place for the most enduring dimensions of early church life. On the Day of Pentecost, the Holy Spirit manifested His presence and power "like the rush of a mighty wind, and it filled all the house where they were sitting" (Acts 2:2). References have already been made to the prominence of homes in the life of the early Christian community (Acts 2:46; 5:42).

This pattern continued throughout the Book of Acts. It was in the home of Cornelius, the Roman centurion of Caesarea, that Peter came with a special message of God, accompanied by a mighty manifestation of God's Spirit, in a significant event which symbolized the emerging response of the Gentiles to the gospel. When the jailer at Philippi responded to the witness of Paul and Silas, "he brought them up into his house, and set food before them; and he rejoiced with all his household that he had believed in God" (Acts 16:34).

The only church congregations described in the New Testament which are designated as having a specific location besides a general geographic one are those which are identified with specific homes. There was such a house church in the home of Priscilla and Aquila. In concluding his message to the Christians at Rome, Paul made special reference to the couple and said, "Greet also the church in their house" (Rom. 16:5). Another house church was in the home of Nympha. In the Book of Colossians, Paul sent special greetings "to Nympha and the church in her house" (4:15). There was also a house church in the home of Philemon. In his letter to Philemon, Paul addressed others besides Philemon, and he made special reference to the house church group connected with Philemon's home: "To Philemon our beloved fellow worker and Apphia our sister and Archippus, our fellow soldier, and the church in your house" (v. 2). The homes were the places where the church was best able to have its worship. They were the places of warm fellowship and meaningful teaching—personal communication at its best.

Much of the spontaneous evangelism which characterized

the early church took place within or grew out of the vitality of these house churches.

The New Testament church was in no sense a building. When the Temple and the synagogues were no longer available to them, the early Christians made no effort to erect any kind of physical structure in which to meet. For their mass meetings, they used whatever was available to them—from spontaneous street meetings to the more planned rental of halls. For their small-group meetings, the home not only met their need but was the most conducive environment to the continuing function of church life.

The apostolic era set the pattern for this dynamic expression of church congregational life, and this pattern prevailed during the first two hundred years of the Christian church.

The Early Christian Centuries

Until the year 200, the house church was the common structural expression of the Christian congregation. There is some evidence that the homes of wealthier members (who were very much in the minority) were used for larger gatherings. However, the homes of the rank and file became the scene of ongoing fellowship and greatly enhanced the sense of community which characterized the early church.

Recent discoveries in the city of Capernaum in Galilee, where Jesus made His headquarters for a while, have provided evidence which has led some to believe that a house church met in what may have been the home of the apostle Peter.[1] In the *Clementine Recognitions* (10:71), there is a reference to Theophilus of Antioch who dedicated his palace as a meeting place for a church.[2]

Other early literary sources throw light on these ancient house churches. One relates to the situation in Alexandria,

Egypt, during the time of Clement. From Clement's descriptions, the school in his home was a supplement to the house church which met there.

Even though the house church had the instruction of the members of the Christian community as one of its basic functions, Clement's special school brought this educational function to an especially high level in Alexandria. However, his "house school" in no way eclipsed the "house church"—indeed, it was the means of preparing persons for entering into the church and its worship. Clement described the house in which the church met as being the home of one of the wealthy members of the congregation.[3]

Two archaeological discoveries which throw light on ancient house churches relate to the present church of Saint Clement in Rome and the remains of a house church in Dura-Europos on the Euphrates. The present church of Saint Clement is built upon the remains of a previous church which has been dated in the fourth century. Beneath this early church edifice are the remains of a house. There is strong evidence this house was in existence in the first century. It is a long-standing Roman Catholic tradition, one which many Protestants have now come to share, that this building is the remains of the house of Clement of Rome who lived in the first century.[4]

The practice of building a church edifice over the house of a church leader has been a common practice. There are, in the city of Rome, some eighteen church buildings which bear the name of their reputed founders, early leaders of the Christian movement in the imperial city.[5] The Saint Clement building is one of these.

It was also common to erect church edifices over locations which had come to be shrines because of some special tradition: the Church of the Nativity in Bethlehem, the Church of the

Holy Carpenter in Nazareth, the Church of the Holy Sepulchre in Jerusalem, the Saint Sargius Church, and the Ancient Coptic Church in the old city of Cairo, the reputed place of hiding for the holy family fleeing the wrath of Herod. Like the special sites over which churches were built, the homes of early church leaders which had housed churches came to be esteemed as virtual shrines. In time, a prominent church edifice was often erected on or over the site.

An even more instructive discovery has been the one made at the ruins of the ancient city of Dura-Europos (modern Salhiyeh) on the Euphrates River in the Syrian desert between Baghdad and Aleppo. A large house, probably owned by a wealthy member of the church, was adapted as a place of worship around the year 230. It appears that two rooms had been made into a chapel seating some one-hundred persons. There was a raised section apparently for the preacher or leader of worship (bishop). In one corner was a baptistry covered by a decorated canopy. The walls contain paintings illustrating such biblical stories as Adam and Eve, David and Goliath, the Good Shepherd, Christ walking on the water, and the wise and foolish virgins.[6]

This fascinating archaeological wonder confirms the impressions gained from early literature that the homes of the wealthy often best served the larger needs of the house churches. It also illustrates a phenomenon which seemed common—the large villalike estates of wealthy Christians which housed churches were often willed to the congregation. These came more and more to be adapted to church use and in time came to function exclusively for such purposes. Another example of a private home which had been adapted as an exclusive church edifice was found around the turn of the century at Priene in Asia Minor.[7]

The Middle Ages

The virtual eclipse of the house church in the Middle Ages had its beginning during the era of Constantine. With the emperor embracing Christianity, the life of the average Christian and the structure of church life were altered radically. Before this, Christianity had been an illegal religion. Worship often had to be in secret. The church was persecuted, and during the reign of some emperors the persecution was extensive and severe. Just after the apostolic era, the church grew by the spontaneous witness of its people, with church leaders playing pastoral roles.

With the reign of Constantine, and especially later with that of Theodosius, Christianity moved from underground worship in catacombs and house churches to an era of great acceptance and favor. This paralleled the full development of the bishopric with the bishops in the great cities such as Rome, Alexandria, Constantinople, and Carthage exercising considerable influence and authority. The power of the church was no longer only in its spiritual strength and vitality but in its ecclesiastical influence and favored political and social position.

The Roman church gradually gained enormous influence and prestige because of the political importance of Rome and because of the tradition of Peter and Paul being connected with its early life. As the church came into favor through Christian emperors, it was able to acquire the property of the catacombs, the earlier burial chambers of the Christian community just outside the city. Churches were built over these catacombs. Numerous large house were also acquired whose upper stories were used as house churches. In time they were adapted as independent church structures.[8]

The bishop, who had earlier been a strong pastoral figure

concerned with the spiritual development of the community of faith, now assumed additional roles as a financial and personnel manager, exerting decisive control of the lower clergy such as presbyters, priests, and deacons. Control of the finances of the churches and the clergy often became an exercise in power because of the vast wealth the church began to acquire under Constantine in the fourth century. With the government subsidies which the bishops received after Constantine, along with the offerings from increasingly affluent churches, church buildings proliferated; and the house churches which had been the symbol of community and spirituality disappeared from the mainstream of structural church life.

The Constantinian and Theodosian eras witnessed the emergence of a distinct church architectural type known as the basilica which replaced the house church as the meeting place of the people of God. Constantine built the basilica of Saint John Lateran in Rome, and with this he symbolized a qualitatively different direction for the church.

The basilica was a rectangular hall with a semicircular niche or "apse" extending out from the small side opposite the main entrance. The entrance opened into the nave with two or four rows of columns depending usually upon the size. The basilica was the forerunner of the cathedral, the Romanesque style which reached its peak in 1150 and the Gothic which reached its peak a century later. This was the church edifice which carried the symbolism of the *church as building and not people* to its highest theological implication.

While the house church tradition was lost to the mainstream of the Roman Catholic Church, the tradition was not lost entirely to Christianity. With the emergence of the diocese around the power of the bishop, a parachurch movement emerged which embodied much of the tradition of the house church: the monastic movement.

The monastic movement strongly resembled the house church tradition, especially in its inception, at the point of its spirituality and rejection of worldly values. It was built around a strong personality who was both a teacher and pastor figure. The simplicity which characterized the movement also followed the house church tradition. Its greatest departure was at the point of its asceticism and practice of celibacy. Monasticism had no place for the family, while the house church was family oriented to the core.

With the house church being lost to the mainstream of church life and with the monastery having no place for the family, the spiritual function of the Christian home and family took a new direction. Religious instruction in the home continued, but it had little or no integral connection with organized church life. Rather, religion in the home continued as a parallel phenomenon to institutionalized church life throughout this period.

The house church tradition also found expression in the sectarian groups which the Roman Catholic Church had come to regard as heretical. An excellent example of these groups was the Waldensians, with whom many evangelicals today would strongly identify. They desired to return to scriptural patterns of belief and practice and came to oppose the authority of the church hierarchy. They lived humble lives and met for simplified worship and fellowship in their modest homes. Donald F. Durnbaugh wrote: "The manuals of the inquisition which describe these heretics for the purpose of apprehension give inadvertent testimony to the quality of life often developed by the medieval sectarians."[9]

In the period just before the Reformation, another group

very similar to the Waldensians appeared in Eastern Europe in what is today modern Czechoslovakia. They were known as the Unitas Fratrum. They assembled in homes to hear the teachings of their leader, Peter Chelvicky, in the 1400s.[10] To some extent, they were the forerunners of other renewal movements which were to emerge in Europe in the next few hundred years.

The Reformation Period

Just as the earlier Roman Catholic bishops had taken over pagan temples, purified them, and adapted them for use in the Latin liturgy, so the Protestant reformers took over Roman Catholic churches, freed them from what they deemed Roman excesses and improprieties, and adapted them to the Reform expressions of worship and polity. The Reform movement, therefore, was almost as bound to the church edifice as the Roman Church.

However, in little-known writings of Luther, the great reformer saw potential in the house church despite the fact that it was associated with the more radical wing of the Reformation, such as the Anabaptists. Luther had a vision of the devout meeting in homes to practice their faith in a depth of expression which was difficult to achieve in the mainstream of church life and practice. This vision seems to have been too ideal for Luther, however, and among his many duties, it apparently did not receive priority."[11]

The house church is best illustrated during this period among the Anabaptists. They had no church buildings but came together in homes for worship and the development of their spiritual community. They met usually four or five times a week in their house church assemblies.[12]

The Post-Reformation Period

Inspired by the earlier Anabaptists, the Church of the Brethren, which grew out of the European Pietist Movement, developed a strong pattern of house church worship. They had an early aversion to meeting houses and interpreted the concept of the church in terms of the gathered community of faith. They deliberately chose to follow the house-to-house meeting patterns of the primitive Christians.

However, like many other renewal groups, they did erect meeting houses by the nineteenth century, but at first they were deliberately very plain and unadorned. Like the Mennonites, descendents of the Anabaptists, their first meeting houses had the appearance of a residence more than that of a traditional church edifice.[13]

The house church movement reached its most definitive expression since the early centuries in Post-Reformation Europe within the Pietist movement. In Germany in the seventeenth and eighteenth centuries, two learned and devout men made a significant impact upon their time and led a movement which had profound implications for the future of Protestant Christianity. They were Philip Jacob Spener and August Herman Francke. They started the *collegio pietatis,* house meetings for prayer, Bible study, and discussion. In 1675 Spener wrote *Pia Desideria, Holy (or Pious) Desires,* in which he developed his ecclesiology of "little church within the church." Because the house church best embodied that concept, Spener's thought is definitive for the house church movement.[14]

The Moravian movement united two profound traditions of Pietism in the eighteenth century. It began when Nikolaus Ludwig Count von Zinzendorf received on his estate a group of refugees from Moravia. Zinzendorf had been tutored by

Francke in the school in his home. He was, therefore, a direct product of this Pietist movement.

The Moravians were descendents of evangelical dissidents who had worked for church renewal for hundreds of years in Eastern Europe. On his estate, Zinzendorf, guided by pietist ecclesiology, led in developing the Moravians into a revolutionary missionary community which profoundly influenced such historical notables as John Wesley and William Carey. From the home of Zinzendorf, the Moravians spread to many parts of the world, carrying their strong personal faith and gathering converts into house groups after the tradition of their teacher, Zinzendorf, and his teacher, Francke.

The Moravians had both an ideological and methodological imprint upon Wesley. Although Wesley had used the small-group approach in his "holy club" even before his famous Altersgate experience, it was through the Moravians that he found the spiritual key—the ecclesiology—that turned this concept into a revolutionary method for evangelism and church growth. This small-group approach was basic to the Wesleyan revival that swept England and later made its impact on America. The so-called neighborhood class meetings which were held in homes were the cornerstone of the Wesleyan methodology. Howard Snyder concluded that "the classes were in effect house churches."[15]

Most modern denominations had their origin in house meetings. This was true of the Baptists and Disciples as well as the Methodists. The Holiness revival that swept the United States the latter part of the nineteenth century and the modern Pentecostal movement which began in the early part of this century had their genesis in home meetings.

The Modern Period

Even though there was some reappearance of the house church in Europe, mostly in England and Scotland, toward the end of World War II, the major development did not come until the 1950s and 1960s. The house church in China, basic Christian communities in Latin America, Jesus Movement house churches, and the explosion of home cell group ministries are the best examples of this recent worldwide trend. But numerous other forms of home-related worship exist, some new and innovative, others with deep roots into the past.

One of the earlier twentieth-century forms of the house church which continues to grow in influence is the Christian Ashram of India. The first Protestant Ashrams emerged in the 1920s, and the first Catholic Ashrams appeared in the 1950s. Although strongly influenced by Western missionaries, the Ashrams are intentionally Indian in style, structure, and purpose. The term *Ashram* is simply an Indian word for *house* and should not be confused with its use in connection with Hindu cults in the United States.

The Ashrams range from the simple Gandhian model of a disciplined community working for social change to the guru-centered model, more spiritual in tone, seeking a more vitally indigenous Christian expression in the Indian context. Both are Christian and have a simple life-style in common, but the goals of the former are more outward and political while the goals of the latter are more inward and communal.[16]

Another form of small-group movement which bears some resemblance to the Christian Ashrams are the Basic Christian Communities of Latin America. They are of Roman Catholic origin and are still a movement within the Roman Catholic

Church. They grew out of a concern for the poor and are essentially a church of the poor.

These communities, which usually meet in the homes of the poor, are a kind of counter church to traditional Roman Catholicism in Latin America. The movement is lay-oriented, though many priests and nuns are sympathetic with it and relate to it in an informal manner. It enjoys growing acceptance among the leadership of the Catholic Church. Its faith is Roman Catholic with a strong liturgical flavor characterizing the home meetings. However, it is radical in its application of faith to the social issues related to poverty and oppression in Latin America. These basic Christian communities have been described as prophetic, missionary, and communitarian. They are like certain Ashrams in that they are a spiritual community seeking social change through nonviolence. This Latin American model has inspired groups elsewhere, and the movement is now gaining some momentum in Africa and such Asian countries as the Philippines.[17]

Since mid-century there has been a strong church renewal movement centering in the house church and stimulated by programs of the World Council of Churches and the National Council of Churches. This movement has been ecumenical in nature. One aspect of the movement has been special studies on the missionary nature of the church, particularly in relationship to the growing younger churches on the traditional mission fields. The movement has led many persons to a new sense of the interdependence of all churches. This church renewal emphasis, expressing itself in various types of house church groups, has spread over the world among many different denominational groups.[18]

Another form of the house church movement which has flourished since mid-century is communitarian in nature and function. They resemble the types of house church communities that go back to the days of the Anabaptists. They have both urban and rural settings, depending upon specific functions of the group. A classic example of this type is the Hutterian Brethren, an Anabaptist group which has had a continuing history of communal living since the early sixteenth century. The Society of Brethren has reunited with this movement in recent years. Similar communal house church groups, totally unrelated to these earlier movements, have grown out of the Jesus movement.[19]

The house church has also assumed a monastic or semimonastic flavor in some Protestant settings. This is not new; such Protestant orders for men and women have been developing for some time, particularly in India and Sri Lanka. One of the newer communities of inspiring vitality which has become famous is at Taize, France. Here, near Cluny, the headquarters for medieval monastic renewal, young people have banded together for prayer and renewal. The community combines the inward values of spirituality with an outward prophetic application to the issues of the day.[20]

Some house church groups today go beyond the traditional pietist orientation of others and use the techniques and insights of transactional analysis and encounter therapy. Sometimes these innovative psychological methods are combined with the more traditional exercises of prayer and Bible Study, often in such a way as to give the traditional exercises new implications for personal growth and social involvement.[21]

Whereas in the past, homes were often used as a beginning point until a new congregation could provide its own traditional facility, more and more house groups are now remaining such by design and are becoming autonomous house churches. They are independent of a host church and may relate to larger denominational units just as the traditional church types do. They are house churches in the truest sense of the term.

Although some house groups come and go, and although traditional churches are still typically bound to their buildings —all over the world in many and varied ways, home worship is thriving, and the momentum is so great there seems to be no sign of abatement.

We now turn our attention to a theology of church structure. In the next chapter we examine church structure in general and Christian house group forms in particular in the light of biblical imperatives and attendant cultural constraints.

Notes

1. *Eerdman's Handbook to the History of Christianity*, ed. Tim Dowley (Grand Rapids: Wm. B. Eerdmans Publishing Co., 1977), p. 58.

2. See Floyd V. Filson, "The Significance of the Early House Churches," *Journal of Biblical Literature* (1939), p. 107.

3. See J. G. Davies, *Daily Life in the Early Church* (London: Lutterworth Press, 1952), p. 25; also Donald R. Allen, *Barefoot in the Church: Sensing the Authentic through the House Church* (Richmond: John Knox Press, 1966), p. 23.

4. See Filson, p. 107.

5. Dowley.

6. Ibid.; see also M. Rostovtzeff, *Dura-Europos and Its Art* (Oxford: Clarendon Press, 1938), pp. 130-134; Allen, pp. 23-24. Filson, pp. 107-108. For an excellent photograph of this house church room, see Dowley, p. 58.

7. Filson, p. 8.

8. Dowley, p. 120.

9. Donald F. Durnbaugh, "Intentional Community in Historical Perspective," *The House Church Evolving*, ed. Arthur L. Foster (Chicago: Exploration Press, 1976), p. 16.

10. Ibid.

11. Ibid., pp. 16-17.

12. Ibid., p. 17-18.

13. Ibid., p. 18-19.

14. Ibid., p. 19-20; see also Dowley, p. 443, and Howard A. Synder, *The Problem*

of Wine Skins: Church Structure in a Technological Age (Downers Grove, Ill.: Inter-Varsity Press, 1975), p. 140.

15. Howard A. Snyder, *The Radical Wesley* (Downers Grove, Ill.: Inter-Varsity Press, 1980), p. 54.

16. See P. O. Phillips, "The Place of Ashrams in the Life of the Church," *International Review of Missions* (vol. XXXV, 1946), p. 265. See also, "Ashrams and Basic Christian Communities." Workshop Paper IV, International Association for Mission Study, Bangalore, India, 4-10 Jan. 1982, pp. IV, 1-3.

17. Ibid.

18. See Durnbaugh, p. 20. See also Hans-Ruedi Weber, "The Church in the House," *Concern*, no. 5 (June 1958), pp. 7-28.

19. Durnbaugh, p. 21.

20. Durnbaugh, pp. 21-22.

21. See Philip and Phoebe Anderson, *The House Church* (Nashville: Abingdon Press, 1975).

3
A Theology of Church Structure

There is a direct line between nature, function, and structure. We can expect the church to assume certain functions growing out of its nature, and we can expect these functions to be translated into structures as the church takes root and grows in its cultural, social, economic, and political context. A theology of church structure, therefore, is the way in which we perceive structural forms as the reflection of the nature of the church and the essential functions which attest to that nature.

The Nature of the Church
in the New Testament

The nature of the church in the New Testament may be understood in two ways: (1) through direct statements on the church; and (2) through descriptions of church life. Paul used a variety of language and thought in his direct teaching on the nature and function of the church. Basic to all was the concept of the church as the possession of God in Christ. It is the church of God (1 Tim. 3:5; 3:15). It is the church of Christ (Rom. 16:16).

These are descriptions of possession in the New Testament and were not formal names of the church, with due respect to the denominational groups which so use these descriptions.

Jesus called the church "my church" (Matt. 16:18). He referred to His disciples, the followers who formed the first nucleus of the church, as "mine" (John 17:10). Earlier, in His discourse on the true Shepherd, He had referred to His followers as "my sheep" (John 10:27).

Paul's letters contain a number of figures of speech to describe the nature and function of the church. A major metaphor is that of a household, a family. This figure conveys an idea which has a deep rootage in the Old Testament where God's people are often referred to in a variety of family-oriented figures. In writing to Timothy, Paul referred to the church as the "household of God" (1 Tim. 3:15). He used the same language in writing to the Ephesian Christians (Eph. 2:19).

In Galatians 6:10, Paul changed the language slightly and referred to the church as the "household of faith." Peter used a similar metaphor in calling the church "a spiritual house" (1 Pet. 2:5) and a "brotherhood" (1 Pet. 2:17), a generic reference, of course.

One of Paul's favorite designations of the church was that of the body of Christ (1 Cor. 12:12-13; Eph. 1:22-23; 2:16; 4:16; 5:23; Col. 1:18-24; 2:19; 3:15). It appears that a major motivation of Paul in using this figure was to illustrate the unity in diversity which characterizes the function of the church.

The analogy also affirms the rightful control of "the body" by "the head" (the mind) which is Christ. Certainly, the body exists to do the will of the head of the body which is Christ. The analogy of the physical body obviously is meant to illustrate the function of the "body politic" (in the basic meaning of that term, not necessarily the modern political meaning in the sectarian sense). Perhaps the phrase "the polity of the body" would best give the ecclesial connotation.

The high place the New Testament affords the church can be

seen in the exalted passages which describe the church as the instrument of God's glory (Eph. 3:21) and the medium of His redemptive purpose (Eph. 3:9-11).

The instrumental nature of the church did not originate with Paul, however, though he did use new imagery to emphasize it. This idea was first enunciated by Jesus Himself in Matthew 16:18-19 when He spoke of the church as possessing the keys of the kingdom. Even more fundamental is the statement, directly missional in nature, in which Jesus linked His mission with the purpose of the church (John 17:18; 20:21). When we connect these definitive words of Jesus with the other commissions (Matt. 28:19-20; Mark 16:15; Luke 24:46-49; Acts 1:8), we are able to see clearly that the ultimate implication of the instrumental nature of the church is that mission is its very nature and function.[1]

Another type of language, one which links the church to the central redemptive theme of the New Testament, describes the church in terms of its origin. In the moving scene in which Paul gave his farewell word to the elders at Ephesus he said: "Take heed to yourselves and to the flock, in which the Holy Spirit has made you overseers, to care for the church of God which he obtained with the blood of his Son" (Acts 20:28).

In His great pastoral discourse, Jesus identified Himself as the true Shepherd who gives His life for His sheep (John 10:15-17). Paul, in his Epistles, emphasized the same concept.

In Ephesians 2 and Colossians 1, Paul said that the church was created out of the reconciling power of the cross. In Ephesians 5, he referred to Christ as the Savior of the body which He loved and for which He gave His life. These passages link the origin of the church—its very existence—with the cross, the heart of the gospel itself.

The Function and Structure
of the New Testament Church

The above biblical material illustrates graphically the theology of the church in the ideological sense—one in which the church is equated with the fellowship of the redeemed. There is, however, another set of biblical materials, more directly descriptive in nature, in which the empirical church is described in all its space-time reality. And the astounding thing we observe is how the church in all of its many manifestations reflects in function the very qualities presented ideologically in the teaching of Jesus, Paul, and others in the New Testament.

A survey of the Book of Acts will demonstrate this convincingly. Acts 2 gives us a considerable amount of data about the function of the Jerusalem Church. First, proclamation was central as is shown by the sermon of Peter on the Day of Pentecost. The evangelism which followed filled the young church with new converts and a fresh spiritual vitality. The inspiring account of the life of the church in the wake of this spiritual revival highlights the functions of the church. These functions may be summarized as follows: (1) attention to the apostles' teaching; (2) fellowship (sense of unity); (3) breaking of bread in the homes; (4) prayers; (5) reverence for, praise to, and rejoicing before God; (6) material sharing; (7) Temple worship; (8) community witness (favor with all the people); and (8) evangelism (daily adding to the church).

The profound sense of God's presence through the Holy Spirit, the mood of reverence, the offerings of prayers and praise, and the rejoicing before God accent the transcendent and other-worldly nature of the community as having its origin in God and as being His very own possession.

The fellowship, sense of unity, and material sharing illustrate the church as a united body in Christ and a caring family of God. The prayers, praise, and rejoicing reflect gratitude for the price paid for their redemption through the cross. If the breaking of bread refers to the Lord's Supper, this link with the cross is even more directly expressed in the worship of the community.

The proclamation and evangelism, the community witness, even the ministry to each other, illustrate the instrumental function of the missional community. The link with the apostles' teaching was crucial because they were the ones who had been with Jesus. They had heard His words concerning the church, and they had received His commission. They were the repository of the gospel message. They had first received from Him the Lord's Supper. They were the firstfruits of the redemptive work of the cross out of which the church was born. "The teaching" is primary and paramount, the first item mentioned in the inspiring catalogue of these first acts of the apostles.

Throughout the Book of Acts, these functions continue as the witness spreads over the Mediterranean world. Some highlights are: the continued sense of being Christ's possession and being on His mission, the sensitivity to the need for unity in the body especially with the growing diversity in the admission of Gentile converts into the family of faith, the prominent place of teaching, the centrality of worship in the development of the body, the power of proclamation in the evangelistic outreach of the community, the priority of ministry (healing and other forms) as an expression of the servant nature of the church.

To summarize, a number of key terms emerge which articulate these functions in reflection of the nature of the church: (1) *didache,* "the teaching," (2) *koinonia,* "the fellowship," (3) *liturgy,* "the worship," (4) *diakonia,* "the ministry," (5) *kerygma,* "the proclamation." Three of these are more inward, that is, they reflect the functions of the church in the deepest elements of communal life in the family of God. They are the didactic function, the koinoniac function, and the liturgic function.

Two of the above are more outward in function, that is, they reflect the missional nature of the church: the diakonic function and the kerygmatic function. As function is translated into structure, the form which emerges is inherently related to the nature of the church. Therefore, a theology of church structure is only an expression of the theology of the church in keeping with the context of the day. In terms of culture, we note the strong Jewish flavor of the church in its initial expression: worship in the Temple, association with the synagogue, and so forth. Also the prominence of the home reflected the high place of religious instruction in the Hebrew family. The emerging prominence of the elder in a leadership role reflected a strong cultural pattern of community leadership. The church experienced its first great burst of spiritual and numerical growth in the context of a Jewish celebration: the feast of Pentecost.

In terms of the social context, the early church was an urban church. Therefore, communication assumed the form of mass expression typical of communication in the public sphere of the city. It also assumed the form of small-group communication, reflecting the primary groups which always constitute the urban mosaic. In terms of the patterns of common life, the early church reflected urban mobility and not the static patterns of rural life. It also tended to be secular in expression, from the beginning not reflecting the patterns typically expressed in traditional religious life.[2]

In terms of economics, the church was predominantly poor —constituted of the common masses. Yet, it did have a prominent minority of the more wealthy members of society, educated persons of considerable standing in the community. The more prominent house churches—the ones identified by the names of the host family or person—seem to have been connected with the residences of these prominent Christian leaders. The mixture of the social classes in the early church caused both blessings and problems: a challenge to liberality of giving and a temptation to make this a measure of spirituality.

In terms of politics, the church was in trouble with the political establishment for the first three-hundred years of its life. In Judea, the church was always in conflict with the Jewish authorities in Jerusalem. This had a profound effect upon what the church was able to do in terms of public structural life. In the Roman Empire, the church was an illegal religion, acknowledging Jesus, not Caesar, as the only Lord. This forced the church to be largely an underground movement much of its early life. This pattern was set in the New Testament era.

In terms of function and ultimately in terms of structure, the New Testament account reflects clearly how the church was able to transcend its cultural, social, economic, and political context; how it was conditioned by that context; and even how it was enhanced by it. Moreover, it was in the house church that we are best able to see this structural reflection of the nature and function of the church in relationship to its environment.

The didactic function of the church could best be performed in the homes. Neither the Temple nor the synagogue were appropriate for this, primarily because of the nature of the teachings which centered in the gospel itself. This was a threat to the leadership of both these religious institutions. Besides this, the family setting, which had been the center for religious teaching and observance from Old Testament times, was more conducive to the communal nature of early church instruction. Even though the early church did have a strong Jewish orientation, it transcended its cultural context in terms of this Jewish element and was able to dictate the terms of its life and function. Even though the Jerusalem Church retained its Jewishness in terms of circumcision and other profound elements of Judaic identification, it was soon separated from the Temple, the synagogues, and the other benefits of the religiocultural establishment of Jerusalem.

The Gentile church was able to move beyond circumcision, sabbath observance, and other long-hallowed Judaic essentials. In both Judaic and Hellenistic traditions, however, the homes became the scene for the development of the distinctively Christian elements in this new community of faith.

Even though the house church reflected aspects of the cultural, social, economic, and political context of which it was a part in both positive and negative ways, the essential nature of the church was not determined by it. Furthermore, the very context of the house church enhanced the function of the church.

We are able to see this in the koinoniac function of the church. The church as the household of God and the household of faith was best able to express itself in the hospitality and fellowship of the Christian home. Though the Jews had their Temple and synagogues and the Gentiles had their pagan temples, in both traditions religious observances had long been largely centered in the homes. In this regard, the house churches were culturally indigenous to both traditions. However, the new house churches brought a distinctively Christian content to the tradition of religious instruction in the home, and it was precisely in the fellowship of the house churches that early Christianity was able to make both a psychological and a theological break with Judaism.

We can explain the preoccupation of Paul with the family largely on the basis of the significance of the house church. On occasions, entire households united with the church as a family unit. This resulted in a special family orientation within the Christian fellowship. The almost total concentration of Christian life in the home resulted in a consistent effort to improve the quality of home life for the Christian family.

This apparently was true for both the larger homes of the more prominent families and the smaller homes of the more modest families. Paul was careful to give strong admonition to each member of the household, beginning with the father and the mother. The spiritual life of the church and the family were inextricably linked in the early house church.

The liturgic function of the early church was best expressed in the house churches. The major ritual or symbol of the church next to baptism was the Lord's Supper. It grew out of the Passover feast, and its first observance was in a home setting. As the Lord's Supper developed, and as it later came to be linked with the *agape* meal, the home was the most appropriate setting for this practice.

The common table, in the center of the room with the community encircling it, gave this religious observance a powerful family and communal orientation. Breaking bread from house to house was the symbol of their communal life. The other liturgical elements of prayer and praise gave a special accent of joy and victory to this spiritual celebration in the homes. The Lord's Supper celebration in the homes was a major way in which there was an affirmation of the priesthood of the believers.

The diakonic function was integral to the early house church. The church was a servant community, sent to minister to the total needs of persons. The church was sent by Christ as He had been sent by the Father (John 17:18; 20:21), so its life was involved in being on mission to minister to human need. This ministry was both within the community and without.

An example of the former is illustrated in the wealthier members sharing with their brothers and sisters (Acts 2) and the appointment of deacons to see that widows of both the Judaic and Hellenistic factions in the church were adequately cared for (Acts 6). The flow of ministry out into the community can be aptly illustrated by the ministries of healing which attended the work of Peter and John (Acts 3, etc.) and those which attended the work of Paul (Acts 19). Though by its very missional nature, ministry was an outward function of the church, it played a significant role in the unity of fellowship in the early church. The closeness of the family-like situation in the house churches made ministry to one another an inherent function of the family of God.

The kerygmatic function was at the heart of New Testament evangelism. Proclamation, therefore, reflected the outward expression of the church and was central to its missional nature. We have noted previously the public aspect of this missional function of the apostolic church. It is at this point that the house church had and has some limitations.

The mass public meetings, without question, enabled the church to give the gospel a greater exposure and make a greater impact for Christianity in society beyond the capability of the usual function of the house church. However, we need to emphasize that some of the homes which hosted house churches— if not most of the central ones—were those of the more prominent and prosperous citizens. Philemon is a good example. Some of these houses could accommodate fair-sized crowds, and there is no doubt that much evangelistic proclamation transpired in these larger house church settings.

Moreover, we must not necessarily associate proclamation

with unusually large crowds after the model of the mass evangelism of Peter, Philip, and Paul in the great public places of the
cities. The kerygmatic function of the early church was the
proclamation of the good news of what God had accomplished
in Christ for the redemption of the world. It was the heart of
the Christian message and teaching. Therefore, there was not
always strict separation between the didactic and the kerygmatic functions in the New Testament as some recent scholars
would have us believe (Acts 4:1-2; 5:42).

Another significant matter about evangelism in the New Testament is that much of it—if not most of the more enduring
type—took place in the house churches. This was true not
simply because the larger homes were able to accommodate the
function. It was also true because proclamation took place as
a result of the total witness of the interrelated functions of
church life in the homes.

John spoke of evangelism in terms of an invitation to community, an invitation to enter the fellowship of the family of God
(1 John 1:3). Moreover, in that sublime passage from the pen
of Paul in Romans 15:16, the apostle spoke of his ministry of
evangelism in strong liturgical language: "to be a minister [lei-
tourgos] of Christ Jesus to the Gentiles in the priestly service
of the gospel of God, so that the offering of the Gentiles [con-
verts] may be acceptable, being sanctified by the Holy Spirit."
In these passages, and in many others in the New Testament,
the interrelatedness of the New Testament functions is clearly
illustrated.

The more inward functions (teaching, fellowship, and worship) are inherently related to each other, as are the more
outward functions (ministry and proclamation). We would add,
however, that the inward and outward functions themselves are
inherently related. The inward functions are the source of the

outward functions, and the outward functions are a reflection of the inward functions.

Even though the missional nature of the early church compelled it to forms of public witness outside the homes as an augmentation to the evangelism which happened there, it was the common life of the house church centered in its teaching, fellowship, and worship which provided the theological and spiritual basis for that witness. The dynamic which made the early church such a vital and effective community of faith was its rootage in the homes.

It is a mistaken notion to conclude that the only reason the apostolic community developed house churches was because it was a persecuted minority and, therefore, could not go public in its institutional expression. As a matter of fact, the early church was quite public in its witness, despite the fact that it was persecuted.

We only need to remember the public ministry of the church leaders who carried the church's witness to the streets and public forums: Peter, Philip, Stephen, and Paul. We may readily concede that being unwelcomed in the Temple and synagogues and being often persecuted as a result of their public witness may have hastened the development of house churches. However, this did not cause their development.

We have noted earlier that the New Testament church was in no sense a building. The apostolic community never entertained this notion. It did not have this static "place" consciousness. Paul was a tentmaker, and he, no doubt, could have built some kind of a tent, perhaps after the model of the Tabernacle, in which to house his ministry, especially in Ephesus where he stayed for two years. But apparently it never dawned on him. It was utterly foreign to the way he and the early Christians thought of the church. The church was the people—first, last, and always.

Therefore, the house church was the center of the administrative principles which guided the church in the New Testament era and beyond. Floyd V. Filson said:

> The development of church polity can never be understood without reference to the house churches. The host of such a group was almost inevitably a man of some education, with a fairly broad background and at least some administrative ability. . . . In a mission movement which required resourcefulness and courage, they were likely candidates for leadership. It was not merely an inherited theory of polity but in part at least the actual leadership provided by the hosts of the house churches which determined the form of church life.[3]

Though the whole question of leadership and polity will be discussed in a later chapter, it is appropriate at this stage to make a few observations. In the apostolic period, it was the apostles who gave general guidance to the life of the house churches: the original eleven under the leadership of James in Judea and Paul in the Gentile world with Peter moving somewhat in both worlds.

There was a certain authority which emanated from their ministries. Otherwise, leadership in the churches centered in the host and/or leader of the house church. A variety of leadership roles and functions existed in the various house congregations: bishops (overseers), pastors, elders, prophets, teachers, and deacons. There may have been some distinction among the functions of bishops, or elders, and deacons; but these roles were not formalized in a definitive way in the New Testament era.

There seems to have been a plurality of leaders in each congregation—certainly in each community of house churches in a given city. Moreover, these titles of leadership often seemed interchangable with the same leaders being designated by more than one title. What seems clear in the New Testament is that next to the apostles themselves, the house church leaders were the most important in terms of the ongoing life of the church. Since there was no actual distinction between clergy and laity in the New Testament and since all leaders had other vocations, it is difficult to distinguish between "minister types" (Priscilla and Aquila) and "lay types" (Philemon and Nympha). No doubt some of the house church leaders were bishops or elders, but certainly not all of them appear to have been.

Theological and Structural Changes in History

There is a continuity between the apostolic church and the church which followed this era up until the time of Constantine —through the house church and the kind of spiritual life which it fostered. For generations after the apostles, the church continued its spontaneous lay (people of God) witness in the cities and along the great trade routes of the empire. However, some ideological changes were taking place which were altering the New Testament theology of the church. The plurality and equality of leadership was giving way to a hierarchical arrangement with the bishop becoming the central figure followed by the presbyters (who later became priests) and deacons. Later, such roles as exorcists and acolytes were added. It appears that after the apostles, the bishops, who were at first pastors, assumed a role of authority as well as leadership. The bishop would have been pastor of a house church; but in time his congregation came to be the central one, and the other house congregations in a given city would then be pastored by presbyters under the authority of the bishop. In a given city, certainly in the Western church, only one pastor in a city could be a bishop.

Other aspects of theological adaptation came with a more sacramental understanding of baptism and the Eucharist. This was one of the forerunners of the beginning division between the clergy and the laity. Additional doctrinal formulations brought new theological perceptions which were to have substantial impact on ecclesiology. This, in time, had profound implications for the function and structure of the church. Though these changes were emerging, the church kept much of its apostolic tradition and identity because of its minority status and because persecution forced the house groups into a deep solidarity of fellowship.

It is a mistaken notion, however, to conclude that the church in this period expressed itself only in the privacy of house groups and such secret places as catacombs. Despite periods of intense persecution, there was impressive growth in parts of the empire. In this period, the whole city of Edessa and the entire nation of ancient Armenia were Christianized. Such areas as Asia Minor, except some of the remote sections, and ancient Thrace had an estimated 50 percent Christian population by the year 300. Besides this, parts of Italy, Syria, North Africa, and Egypt had sizable minority populations of Christians.[4]

The most definitive change for the nature, function, and structure of the church came with Constantine. With his acceptance of Christianity, the church came into public favor. Perhaps nothing symbolized this change as dramatically as the shift from the house church to the basilica as the fundamental expression of church life and function. Worship in the house church had affirmed and symbolized the priesthood of all believers and the unity of the body in one fellowship of the people of God. Moving into the basilica was more than a changing of meeting place. It symbolized a change in the very nature of church life and function. This meant a change in ecclesiology—in the theology of church. The basilica facilitated the division between the clergy and laity and gave it definitive support and formal expression. Worship changed from being the united celebration of all the people to a clergy-performed ritual with the laity as spectators. It was a fundamental and qualitative departure.

The basilica, by its very structure and design, represented in a concrete, visible form the changes in the theology of the church.[5] It was a design which dramatized the differences in God's people as vividly as the house church had expressed their unity and oneness. The "apse" was the domain of the clergy. In the center of this area was a thronelike chair in which the bishop sat—depicting more of a power image than a pastoral one. The table for the Lord's Supper was in the front of the apse, in the area which later came to be known as the altar. The nave, in the center of the basilica, was occupied by the "lower" clergy and the choir. The people, the "spectator-worshipers," were relegated to the side aisles, separated by gender. The catechumens (those under instruction for church membership) and the penitents (those under the discipline of the church) were restricted to the porch area near the outer area of the nave.[6]

This building-centered structure of the church has dominated institutional church life ever since. The basilica in the Roman church later was followed by the cathedral and in time a plethora of related church-edifice types, varying in peripheral architectural design but retaining the essential pattern set in the Constantinian era. The Orthodox Church has followed much the same tradition. The Protestant denominations have all been influenced by this early pattern at a few definitive points. Whether apse or pulpit area, altar or platform—the clergy and laity are separated by design. The clergy and related types lead, officiate, perform, etc., but the people are still often spectator-worshipers. Even in the new circular auditoriums or sanctuaries where the people come closer, there is still a clear line of demarcation between the clergy and the laity in the design. Some changes have taken place. The choir in the more liturgical churches is in the balcony and in the less liturgical ones in the loft behind or beside the pulpit. But this symbolism has only slightly changed the spectator orientation of the people. Congregational forms and other types of church structure have also helped create audience participation, but the fundamental design and function still remain.

It has been in the great renewal groups that an effort to recover both the nature and function of the church in terms of structure has occurred. Whether it has been the Waldensians before the Reformation, the Anabaptists during the Reformation, or the Brethren groups after the Reformation, there has been a striking similarity—the recovery of the priesthood of the believer, the blurring of lines between the clergy and the laity, an emphasis on the unity and oneness of all the people of God, and the recovery of the house church.

Implications for Theology and Structure Today

The book and movie *I Heard the Owl Call My Name* is a moving story about a young priest who was dying of an incurable disease. His mentor and spiritual father advised him to take as his first pastorate a ministry among the Indians of the great Northwest. He, himself, had served there as a young man, and he felt that the quality of spiritual life among these native Americans would provide the young priest with the support he was going to need for the ordeal which was ahead of him. When he arrived by boat at his destination, the priest was warmly greeted by the people. As he moved inland and came over a knoll, his eyes caught something special, and he remarked, "My first church." It was the church edifice. He had already been with the people, but it was only when he saw the building that he said, "My first church." This is typical of the "edifice complex" which most Christians possess in their understanding of the church.

It is common when new congregations are preparing to build their first church edifice to hear someone say, "I hope we build a church that looks like a church." They obviously are not thinking of a New Testament image of the church—but as a matter of fact are reacting against the very plain edifices many evangelical churches have erected.

It is also common in visual aids promoting church extension or planting to see church buildings illustrated by colonial or modified Gothic types of architecture. Seldom, if ever, are churches depicted as the people, worshiping or doing anything else that churches do. This is done partly perhaps because it is simply easier from a graphics perspective. However, one suspect that a church building would more readily say "church" than any kind of people-oriented illustration. This is probably true in the mind both of the illustrator and the audience with whom he or she is communicating.

We have inherited this edifice complex from centuries of church history. Even the so-called fourth force, the Holiness and Pentecostal denominations, has fallen into the same pattern.

It is true that the architecture and arrangement of the sanctuary or auditorium and its furnishings reflect the theology of respective groups. The prominence of the altar reveals a more liturgical orientation with the Eucharist at the center of worship. The prominence of the pulpit, especially at the center of the platform, symbolizes the centrality of the Bible and the proclamation of the Word. The divided chancel reflects an effort at balancing the liturgical and the kerygmatic functions.

Baptist churches, in recent years, have brought the baptistry into a prominent place, usually behind the pulpit, to signify the symbolic importance of that ordinance. Historically, the baptistry was usually in the front of the church edifice, certainly in the Western and Roman traditions. The Lord's Supper table, usually situated in front of the pulpit, likewise affirms the importance of that ordinance. Other than the Lord's Supper table in front of the pulpit and the baptistry behind it, there may be little other liturgical symbolism in a Baptist church or any of the other nonliturgical churches.

To those with a liturgical orientation, some Baptist, Holiness, and Pentecostal church auditoriums appear to be more like entertainment halls than worship sanctuaries, with the microphone and musical instruments being much more visible than objects they would identify as relating to worship. Conversely, Baptists and Pentecostals may view the worship aids of the liturgical churches as distracting and as a substitute for free expressions of worship. The point is that all traditions have their symbols and rituals that speak to how the church building formalizes, consciously and unconsciously, the meaning of church for them.

In the move from the house church to the church building, many church groups over the years have tried in varying ways to preserve the small-group aspect as an integral part of church life. Rural churches were usually small enough to preserve this in their basic structure. As the church was urbanized, the lower classes often preserved this small-group identification in storefront churches. This is still a dominant church structure in the inner cities.

The middle classes, who built larger edifices to house larger congregations, preserved the small group through the Sunday School classes. This has been a basic pattern of Southern Baptist churches and, traditionally, the source of much of their growth. Their church edifices in urban areas have usually been built with prominent educational facilities to accommodate this methodology.

What is missing in the Sunday School is a commitment to the essence and centrality of group life. Sunday School is an adjunct or a supplement to the communal life of the family of God. Usually graded by age and separated by gender, the family unit is divided. Often the school is too cognitive in its almost exclusively didactic setting. It is not liturgical in design, mood, or purpose. Some groups do achieve various levels of fellowship through class socials. But perhaps the Wednesday night "pot luck" that brings the family units together in a more communal setting better preserves this traditional sense of the church as family.

There is little doubt that we have lost something vital and precious in our building-oriented church life. Howard Snyder has pointed out some alarming implications of our edifice complex in what he calls the negative witness of our church buildings. They are a witness to: (1) our immobility, (2) our inflexibility, (3) our lack of fellowship, (4) our pride, and (5) our class divisions.[7] Of course, many would disagree; but if we are objective, we must admit that there is some truth in these charges, and some have serious implications for the very nature of the church.

Partly growing out of the problems mentioned above, and partly growing out of a deep surge of renewal, house churches and other expressions of worship in the home have proliferated in recent years. As we observe their effectiveness the world over, these impressive facts loom large: (1) their appeal to people who would probably never relate to traditional edifice-oriented churches, at least initially, (2) their ability to give to people a level of spiritual satisfaction and purpose they had never found in traditional structures, and (3) their incredible evangelistic potential when so oriented.

If we care about people, if we desire to reach them for Christ and His church, if we are concerned about the quality of spiritual life in our churches—then we need to be open to what is happening in Christian house groups. If we care about the Kingdom, if we have a concern for "the cause" beyond our own private religious world—then we need to consider the potential of the house groups.

Sheer pragmatics should open our eyes to the limitation of trying to keep up with our growing world purely through the traditional method of buying property and building church buildings. The future will belong to those who will be able to break the spell of the edifice complex.

However, there must be a higher motivation. What about the stewardship of lavishing all this wealth on ourselves when there is such staggering need around the world? Is this really "our" money? Is it not a fundamental maxim of biblical truth that God is the absolute (certainly ultimate) Owner of all things, and we are His stewards answerable to Him for how we use *all* that He has entrusted to us?

Where is our missional vision—for our communities, our cities, our nation, and our world? What of those who will never be touched by the love of Christ because so much of our money, energy, and interest is locked up in our own little private world within the walls of our church buildings.

Besides, the house church model is not somebody's wild

dream: it is an effective means which is reaching and renewing persons and communities around the world.

What is needed is a strategy in which house groups are used both as a way to reach out in new effort and also as a supplement to and/or a combined method with traditional approaches. We are not going to abandon sixteen-hundred years of history of being and doing church in church buildings, despite all the negative aspects of the edifice complex.

What is needed is a more responsible use of our buildings, through the whole week, for the church and the community. In building new structures, we need to plan for "warmer" and more "welcoming" structures which have greater utility in terms of service to the total needs of the church family and community. Aesthetics need not be sacrificed, but beauty should be achieved more in harmony with such biblical principles as simplicity and serviceability. Church buildings need not be either austere or monuments to our pride.

Moreover, in planning strategies for emerging new areas, wisdom and spirituality would suggest that we plan for the development of house churches in addition to the usual purchasing of sites for new work. The churches today which seem to be most effective are those which have been able to use their traditional church facility as a base from which satellite ministries are projected into the community. This, at least, moves away from the captivity of the edifice complex. Moreover, it accents a vital New Testament principle which characterized the house churches—flexibility.

In the final analysis, there is no one structure which is sacred or ultimate. Even the New Testament churches appropriated a variety of settings and employed a variety of approaches in public proclamation of the gospel and ministry to the people. Moreover, not even the house churches or home meetings were all alike. They varied in size, setting, and leadership. The three most discernable New Testament church models—Jerusalem, Antioch, and Ephesus—were all urban churches but differed greatly in terms of styles of leadership, meeting place, emphasis, and outreach methodology.

What is needed is that which translates the church most authentically in terms both of the essential nature of the church and the indigenous nature of the social context in which the church is planted. Because the house church biblically and historically has been the structure through which this has happened in a vital way and because it gives evidence of being the structure through which it is happening again today, we must be prayerfully open to this prospect as we plan for God's work in the future, both locally and beyond.

Notes

1. See Francis M. DuBose, *God Who Sends* (Nashville: Broadman Press, 1983), pp. 105-107.

2. See DuBose, *How Churches Grow in an Urban World* (Nashville: Broadman Press, 1978), pp. 43-57.

3. Floyd V. Filson, "The Significance of the Early House Churches," *Journal of Biblical Literature,* vol. 58, (1939), pp. 111-112.

4. See Adolph Harnack, *The Expansion of Christianity in the First Three Centuries,* vol. II, trans. and ed. James Moffat, (New York: G. P. Putnam's Sons, 1905), pp. 452-468.

5. See chapter 2 for a description of the basilica.

6. See Tim Dowley, *Eerdmans' Handbook to the History of Christianity* (Grand Rapids: Wm. B. Eerdman's Publishing Co., 1977), pp. 150-52 for a description of the basilica along with photographs and illustrations.

7. Howard A. Snyder, *The Problem of Wine Skins* (Downers Grove, Ill.: Inter-Varsity, 1977), p. 72.

4

Types of Christian House Groups

Are most Christians aware that the growth of house groups has reached the proportions of an international movement, or that many churches now have home-cell groups handbooks or manuals which include the development of specific policies, procedures, and training materials on how to organize and maintain such groups? Probably not. One reason is that these groups exist in many forms and may not appear to be part of the same phenomenon.

An earlier study on this subject suggested that house groups "exist in an almost unlimited variety of expressions."[1] Nonetheless, certain forms of house groups may be more familiar because of efforts to convince other churches of their validity. Lawrence Richards and Paul Y. Cho,[2] for example, advocate the use of small cell groups to accomplish rapid church growth and renewal. This method draws upon a biological model of cell growth in living organisms. The body of Christ, like the literal human organism, achieves growth through cell division and reproduction.

Richards, a former Wheaton College graduate-school professor, advocated a total organizational restructuring of churches through "growth cells," in his book *A New Face for the Church.* Through the development of small-group meetings in homes, responsibilities of nurture and outreach are placed upon all believers thus recreating conditions in which New Testament principles of ministry are said to function most efficiently. In short, the smaller size invites closer fellowship and facilitates integration of new members into the group more effectively than large gatherings.

In a more recent work which has received considerable attention (*Successful Home Cell Groups*), Paul Y. Cho outlined the history and development of the home cell groups. The thrust of his book is to introduce a successfully tested model of church growth through cell groups in Seoul, Korea. In Cho's model, each group is formed in a local neighborhood or community with its own house group pastor but is structurally tied to a central church. Groups that grow to be larger than fifteen active families are required to subdivide and reproduce. Cho now has fifty-thousand home cell groups. He pastors the largest church in the world, Yoido Full Gospel Church, with over half-a-million members.

Similarly, Robert Girard has written about the successful experimentation with small home groups (Christian Home Unit Meetings) in Scottsdale, Arizona. Acting on the ideas of Richards, Girard literally reorganized his church around house groups, eliminating many traditional programs which he considered ineffective (for example, midweek services, women's society, Sunday night services). While some programs like Sunday School were not immediately abandoned, the eventual goal was to "phase out all meetings and organizations other than the growth cells and the Sunday congregational meeting."[3] Girard feels that the home groups are the solution to many problems facing the church today.

Using a somewhat different approach, Ralph Neighbour has designed a fairly sophisticated method for developing

"TOUCH-point" groups or fellowships.[4] Neighbour contends that evangelism cannot proceed without *relationships.* Touch-point groups meeting in homes are intended to build relationships as a vehicle for reaching persons outside the church. Essentially, it is held that persons who feel uncomfortable in a traditional church may be reached easier in a non-traditional setting. There are already hundreds of such groups organized through Touch Ministries, a Houston-based organization that has worked with several denominations to promote the concept.

Philip and Phoebe Anderson outlined a house church theory in their book, *The House Church.*[5] Philip Anderson is a professor of pastoral theology at Chicago Theological Seminary, and Phoebe Anderson is a former assistant professor of education at Chicago State University. Their model draws heavily from humanistic psychology and is aimed at facilitating face-to-face communication and meeting individual needs within a small-group context.

Another study suggests three general types of house church groups: (1) autonomous house churches, (2) federated house congregations, and (3) satellite home fellowships. Autonomous house churches are independent groups not structurally tied to other congregations. Federated house congregations are described as "semi-independent church groups which function separately, with their own pastors . . . and have their own meetings and activities, yet relate in a definitive way to one or more similar groups."[6] Satellite home fellowships are structurally tied to a central church body though they may differ widely in content and style.

David Chancey described the development of "indigenous satellite units" within blue-collar neighborhoods in Fort Worth, Texas, basically as mission-type churches.[7] These house groups were also designed to reach people not comfortable in traditional church settings. The house churches he studied remained a permanent part of a sponsoring church. However, they were expected eventually to become self-sufficient and responsible for their own growth. J. V. Thomas, church extension coordinator for the Baptist General Convention in Texas said, "Ideally, it [the house church] is self-supporting, self-governing, self-multiplying."

Charles Olsen, conducting research through the Project Base Church in Atlanta, has suggested as many as seven different types or models of house churches. These are summarized as follows:[8]

(1) *The Overlay House Church*—The house church is in addition to the regular programming.
(2) *The Vehicular House Church*—This type of house church is the primary vehicle of program and ministry.
(3) *The Para-Base House Church*—Members attend a different church on Sunday while developing an interdenominational base for other activities.
(4) *The Satellite House Church*—This type is comprised of people who are not part of an established congregation but accountable to it.
(5) *The Cluster House Church*—This type forms a cluster of house groups which are connected in some manner.
(6) *The Solo House Church*—This group forms an independent congregation. It may have a denominational affiliation or may not.
(7) *The Chain House Church*—Each church relates to at least two others in a connectional system.

Several of Olsen's types are simply different names for groups already discussed. For example, the "Overlay House Church" is essentially a home cell group, and the "Satellite House Church" is nearly identical to the indigenous satellite unit identified by Chancey. Furthermore, it would appear that some of

Olsen's types are not sufficiently distinct as to deserve a separate type-description. Herein lies the problem.

What unifies the various groups we have discussed is their common intent to organize into small, intimate fellowships, to meet in informal settings such as homes, apartments, or comparable rented facilities, and to draw their members from the local community. But one will invariably encounter such different names for these groups as "satellite home fellowships," "outreach fellowship groups," "home cell groups," "Christian home unit meetings," "growth cells," "koinonia groups," "home Bible studies," "Neighborhood Home Groups," "TOUCH-point groups," "indigenous satellite units," "overlay house churches," "chain house churches," and so on. The terms themselves often lack any uniform definitions and, consequently, can be very confusing to even the most careful observer. Yet these forms do follow a pattern, despite the somewhat arbitrary labels given to them.

Our study of house groups suggests that they can be clustered effectively into five different types. These may be distinguished by a number of relatively distinct, identifiable social and organizational characteristics. The following categories are to the best of our knowledge, a reasonably accurate description of the types of house groups which exist today. They are: (1) the home Bible study, (2) the home fellowship/share group, (3) the home cell group, (4) the base-satellite unit, and (5) the house church. Tables 1 and 2, on the following page, summarize the organizational and leadership characteristics of each type. We use these diagrams as a basis for an in-depth examination and analysis.

The Home Bible Study Group

Some may object to the inclusion of a home Bible study as one type of house group. But our research indicates that often such groups function as much more than Bible studies. They bring people together for prayer, teaching, dialogue, fellowship, and, moreover, they serve as a source of commitment and identity. Many churches have weekly home Bible studies for their members. What distinguishes the home Bible study from other types of house groups is that they tend to be more cognitively oriented. That is, they are primarily designed to instruct in doctrine and theology and thus strengthen one's *knowledge* of Scripture. Social interaction and the development of inter-

Table 1

Leadership Structure of Christian House Groups

Group Type	*Always with designated pastor/leader*	*May be without designated pastor/leader*
Home Bible study		X
Home Fellowship		X
Home cell group	X	
Base-satellite unit	X	
House church	X	

Table 2

Organizational Structure of Christian House Groups

Group type	*Always tied to "host" church*	*not always tied to "host" church*
Home Bible study		X
Home fellowship		X
Home cell group	X	
Base-satellite unit	X	
House church		X

personal relationships are secondary to the instrumental purpose of studying the Bible and anchoring one's beliefs. For example, there is rarely any emphasis on activities that are specifically designed to create intimacy or community, though these are often by-products of the group meetings.

The primary orientation of the Bible study is to seek information and enlightenment rather than to foster *koinonia*. However, a certain identity and commitment toward one another is sealed in the common purpose of studying the Bible together. The discovery of new ideas or beliefs, the adoption of a doctrinal teaching, or the exchange of ideas and positions are all a part of the communication process that enhances sociation and creates what sociologists have called the "ideological primary group."[9]

Ideological primary groups "are informal, unstructured collectivities sufficiently small for members to have direct, face-to-face relations and for each member to have an opportunity to participate at every meeting. They typically consist of from five to fifteen people who meet on a regular basis, usually once or twice weekly, to discuss and analyze common problems and experiences."[10]

All members of such a group normally agree on the proper perspective for defining reality—in this case a biblically oriented perspective. But even so, there are many different levels or avenues of *interpretation*. It is precisely in the collective task of interpretation that individuals are integrated into the group, that a group identity is formed. In the home Bible study, members are engaged in the discovery and development of a shared theology and belief system. Through this process, there emerges a serious conviction and dedication to a central perspective.

Unlike other house groups (for example, home cell groups), home Bible studies may or may not be attached to a host church. Members may belong to or attend different churches while remaining committed to the home Bible study during the week. In some cases, these groups are generated by a single host church and intended primarily for its own congregation. However, home Bible study groups do not have to be satellite units or subgroups of a central church, and, indeed, often they are not. Home Bible studies may evolve from associations in the work setting, from interdenominational efforts (World Home Bible League) and parachurch organizations aimed at college students (Inter-Varsity, Campus Crusade for Christ, Navigators), local street ministries, coffee houses, or friendship networks in the neighborhood or community.

In addition, Bible studies have been used by many denominations to start new churches. In such cases a church planter will begin several Bible studies which will eventually be merged to form a single church. In many (but not all) cases the home Bible studies will then be discontinued. Home Bible studies are often loosely structured and may be leaderless or may at least share leadership responsibilities. On university or college campuses, for example, Bible studies may be held in dormitory rooms, and the participants may rotate responsibilities for teaching or leading a lesson. Organizations like Campus Crusade for Christ and Navigators publish their own materials which assist groups in the systematic study of the Bible. Indeed, Campus Crusade for Christ publishes a manual (*Lay Trainee's Manual*) and Inter-Varsity Fellowship has developed a handbook which includes instructions on how to conduct evangelistic home Bible studies.[11]

House groups which are rooted in a host church may or may

not designate a leader. In some instances, these decisions are left up to the group or to the persons whose home is being used. When the leader is the person whose home is being used, a change of locations may also include a change of leadership. However, house groups attached to a host church are more likely than others to designate a leader of the Bible study. Leaders are frequently elders, deacons, or staff persons in the local church who, in turn, are subject to the informal overview of a pastor or clergyman. This assures the local church of some control over the content of doctrine and theology.

A study of one national organization promoting home Bible studies illustrates an example of groups not structurally tied to host churches. Reach Out Incorporated, headquartered in Chattanooga, Tennessee, claims to have thirty-five thousand members enrolled in their "Precepts on Precepts" home Bible study groups. Training leaders representing the organization are stationed in various cities across the country and offer both fifteen- and thirty-week courses in intensive home Bible study.

Training leaders are basically responsible for helping groups get started and for providing information and materials. However, once they are under way, the home Bible study groups are leaderless and rely on the study book to guide them through the lessons. Each book is a separate study of a selected book in the Bible. Interviews with local staff personnel in one Southern city suggest that weekly lessons require at least two hours of preparation. According to this source, home meetings usually include about fifteen or sixteen people in regular attendance. Participants pay a fee to cover the cost of the books—thirteen dollars for a short course (fifteen weeks) and twenty dollars for a long course (thirty weeks). Courses help leaders start a home Bible study, and the group may opt to continue independently after the course ends. However, information obtained from the interviews suggests that most groups remain with the program and simply proceed to a new book. Originally, the organization began as an effort to form women's Bible studies, though it has now evolved to include separate courses for men and couples.

Denominational organizations also offer programs for developing home Bible studies. For example, the United Methodist Board of Discipleship is exploring the use of informal home meetings for Bible study, according to one spokesperson there. Also, The Sunday School Board of the Southern Baptist Convention is promoting a program called the Outreach Bible Study designed to provide home Bible studies for unreached or unchurched persons. It is being offered as an alternative to conventional church services for persons who, by their own special situation or choice of life-style, are oriented away from church. Similar efforts are being instituted by other denominations as well. In effect, many denominational leaders are becoming increasingly aware of the need to seek flexible alternatives to conventional forms of ministry.

The Home Fellowship/Share Group

Home share groups differ from home Bible studies in several important ways. Primarily, they are likely to have a much greater emphasis on the development of close, interpersonal relationships and community (*koinonia*). Unlike home Bible study groups which are more cognitively oriented, the goals of a home share group tend to be aimed more at fellowship and mutual concern for its members. These house groups seek to create and sustain emotionally satisfying relationships within both the larger religious and secular worlds. "One of the major problems of society today," Cho observed, "is the depersonalization of human beings. . . . This problem has also found its way into many of our churches, particularly the large ones."[12]

Home share groups are organized attempts to combat impersonal, bureaucratic structures that obstruct the building of intimate relationships and the practice of brotherly/sisterly love. Anderson and Anderson argued that through such house groups "persons can create and participate in a loving, caring community beyond any they have known, given the opportunity and leadership. Small face-to-face group meetings . . . get past the superficiality and unimportance of much of what they have heretofore experienced in churches to relationships of depth and meaning and concern."[13]

These groups approximate the traditional sociological concept of a primary group. Primary groups are "characterized by face-to-face interaction and cooperation."[14] In the religious setting, life in the primary group gives rise to shared expectations and ideals as they spring from similar experiences and beliefs. Philip Reiff noted, in the introduction to Charles H. Cooley's classic work *Social Organization,* that the primary group is a manifestation of society's "search for love."[15]

In primary groups, "we really make them [other members] a part of ourselves and identify our self-feeling with them."[16] Religious primary groups such as a home fellowship can offer a more or less stable support structure from which to share one's problems and joys with other like-minded believers in an increasingly secular and impersonal society. In the group dynamics of sharing needs for prayer, comfort, or counseling, individuals may be fused together by familiarity and friendship. Girard contended that the purpose of the home group meeting is "for soul-fellowship, for problem-solving, mutual care, and sharing life in Christ together."[17]

Of course, not all home fellowship groups achieve the status of a primary group. We use the term *approximate* in order to convey the occasional unrealized ideals of some groups. Too often, it is the case that they lack the leadership or the commitment of members to evolve into a primary group. It is possible that the relatively loose structure of such groups could serve as an obstacle to building the kind of commitment that is requisite for a primary group. Cooley contended that love and fulfillment in the primary group is developed through sacrificial action. "One is never more human, and as a rule never more happier," he stated, "than when he is sacrificing his narrow and merely private interest to the higher call of the congenial group."[18] Following Cooley, sociologist Rosabeth Kanter argued that groups which are organized to encourage sacrifice of their members are more likely to endure.[19]

Home fellowship/share groups also differ from home Bible studies in their activities. For example, intensive Bible study may not always be on the agenda for a home share-group meeting. Frequently, such groups meet to share or discuss personal or intimate problems, to pray for each other's needs, or simply to enjoy shared interests and activities together. Meetings may also include some singing or worship. Because of their loose structure, however, home share groups may meet on occasion without any agenda or plan. In other words, these types of groups may decide to meet even in the absence of any deliberate preparation for the meeting. The opportunity to fellowship offers sufficient incentive to convene in and of itself.

With regard to organization, home share groups may or may not be tied to a host church. Like home Bible studies, our research suggests that both types can function effectively. Home share groups tend to meet during the week for several hours at night. In addition, home share groups often function without a designated leader. The idea of "TOUCH-point groups" advocated by Neighbour is an illustration of home share groups. Neighbour recommended allowing the group to be their own leader.

> The best suggestion for leading a small group is: DON'T!
> Don't be the "leader"; don't have a teacher; you may not even
> need an "expert." Let the Lord do the work *through the entire
> group*.[20]

Neighbour suggested that each person in the small group be a catalyst to promote the work of the Holy Spirit in persuading nonbelievers. For Neighbour, TOUCH-point groups are primarily a method of laity outreach to the unchurched and, secondarily, a source of nurture to believers. However, our research of groups in the San Francisco area indicates that, in practice, there tends to be at least equal weight given to nurture and fellowship of believers. Moreover, this does not appear to impede the groups' effectiveness in recruiting unbelievers inside or outside the church.

Richards, among others, argued that the most effective tool of evangelism is "the face-to-face demonstration of love" within the fellowship of believers.[21] Critical outsiders, he contended, are more affected by what they see firsthand than what they may hear as empty words. Richards cited several cases wherein unbelievers are effectively evangelized as a result of the small group's demonstration of love and mutual care.[22] Similarly, material from the Church Extension Division of the Home Mission Board (SBC) identifies the "Outreach Fellowship Group" as an effective way to feed new prospects into the church and its programs.

Another illustration of home share groups may be found in the work of Robert Girard, pastor of Our Heritage Wesleyan Church in Scottsdale, Arizona. Girard credits the influence of

Richards for the successful implementation of small groups to resurrect an apathetic, suburban church. Girard openly embraced the model as "revolutionary" and described how the experimental use of "Christian Home Unit Meetings" transformed his entire theology in *Brethren, Hang Loose.* The book has had wide appeal and is now in its sixteenth printing. Girard estimated the number of home unit meetings in operation at about forty.[23]

Girard's description of house groups led us to classify them as home fellowship/share groups, instead of home cell groups, for the following reasons. First, they were characterized by a looser structure than home cell groups (as reflected in the title of his book). No particular format or structure was imposed upon the group except to give it a goal of "becoming united through the work of the Holy Spirit." This was apparently done in order to prevent stifling the group's freedom of movement. The following comments by Girard supported this observation.

> Each group, we were learning, has a personality of its own. Trying to put every group into the same pigeon hole, may stifle its uniqueness and freedom to follow the Spirit's plan to meet the peculiar needs of the people in each individual group.[24]

In addition, Girard sought to emphasize the "experimental" nature of these groups to the participants, thus suggesting a more flexible form than what is evidenced by the home cell group meetings. "Again," said Girard, "the *experimental* nature of the group was stressed. In six weeks the group would end, unless *they* wanted it to continue."[25]

A second reason for assigning these groups to the category of home fellowship/share groups is the fact that many were "leaderless." Girard commented that, in most cases, "the *group* leads, teaches, counsels, and 'polices' itself, making all its own decisions on a consensus basis."[26] The leadership criterion employed here derives from our use of Cho's model of home cell groups, which is characterized by delegated house church pastors or leaders. In other words, the delineation is simply that home fellowship/share groups may be leaderless while home cell groups are not. This has certain implications for the organizational dynamics of house church groups which we will discuss shortly.

The third reason for placing Girard's home unit meetings in this category is due to the fact that members of the home unit meetings could belong to other churches.[27] Unlike home cell groups which are structurally tied to a host church and serve to pastor their own members, home fellowships may take in persons outside the local church body. While both are evangelistic and invite newcomers, the home fellowship/share group places no expectations on persons to join the church.

The same principle of cell division, however, did operate among the home unit meetings as described by Girard. He outlined the following guidelines for cell division and reproduction.

> When a group reaches more than twelve, some will stop talking and just listen. They will not share, they will only *receive.* (It's like Sunday morning church again!) As the size of the group reaches fourteen or more, some will begin to feel that the group is not meeting their needs or doesn't really need their contribution any more, so they will become irregular in attendence and then simply drop out altogether.
>
> The most effective group size is seven to twelve people. We will start a little church with as few as three.
>
> When a group grows to thirteen active members, it should pray about starting a second group. A new little church can be formed by simply dividing the present group in two. This can

sometimes be done on the basis of geography, if the group is willing.

One of the best suggestions is for the little church to look upon the new group to be formed from them as an "outreach," not as a "division." After discussing the need for a second group and the reasons for it, they should pray that the Holy Spirit would place it on the hearts of some members to volunteer to be the nucleus of a new little church. The "old" group would "mother" the new one, through prayer, encouragement and moral support.[28]

Before entering a discussion of home cell groups, a final word should be said about the distinction between home Bible studies and home fellowship/share groups. The latter type of group will frequently engage in Bible study and make this a regular activity in the small-group meeting. However, the home fellowship group is concerned with the *practice* (not merely the study) of biblical principles of love and community as well. That is, they are conscious, or are made conscious, of being an integrated body, knit together with other believers. The extent to which we are trying to distinguish between cognitive and affective orientations may be overstated in order to clarify the distinction for the reader. Yet, the distinction is real enough to be recognized by others. The following remarks by Girard, for example, illustrate this idea with regard to a house group that failed.

> Another group kept going for more than two years, in spite of the fact that they never learned to share Life together. It was a Bible study—little more. It rejected its role as "the Body," as priests to one another. Its members refused to get "that involved" with one another. Its discussions were mainly on the "idea" level rather than a personal level. I was amazed that it could keep going for so long with no more visible life than it had. But eventually, it dwindled to the two or three who were responsive to the Spirit, and then, graciously, the Spirit built a whole

new group on the old foundation. But the old, impersonal group had to die.[29]

Obviously, many home Bible studies are not impersonal. But the above comments show that a strict emphasis on cognitive aspects, without regard for other spiritual needs of the body, may be detrimental.

The Home Cell Group

Home cell groups are more tightly organized versions of home fellowship/share groups. They are always tied to a central or host church which sponsors and oversees them. This model is based primarily on Cho's work. But the cell-group format has been emulated by literally hundreds of churches in the United States. Some of the more successful ones include Full Gospel Tabernacle, Orchard Park, New York, with over two-hundred home cell groups and about two-thousand participants; Church on the Way, Van Nuys, California, with seventy-five home cell groups and approximately fourteen-hundred participants; Elmbrook Church in Milwaukee with fifty-nine home cell groups and approximately eleven-hundred participants; and Willow Creek Community Church in Chicago with over one-hundred home groups and approximately six-hundred persons involved.

Home cell groups tend to be aimed at persons within the local church body. However, they are typically evangelistic to the extent that individuals in the group are oriented toward outreach. For example, Cho referred to home cell groups as the key to evangelism.

Our church, . . . carries out evangelism primarily through the home cell group system. Each cell group becomes a nucleus of revival in its neighborhood, because the cell group is where real *life* is to be found in that neighborhood. When a home cell meeting is full of life, and when people are happy and sharing their faith and witnessing to what the Lord had done in their lives, other people are drawn to them. Unbelievers become curious.[30]

As seen by Cho's comments, home cell groups basically attract persons through example or "life-style evangelism." If the small group is functioning correctly, the transforming experience of genuine *koinonia* in the life of the believers spills over into contacts in the neighborhood and the workplace. New persons are evangelized by what they observe and experience when brought by friends to the meeting.[31] Outreach or evangelism, then, tends to rely less on marketing techniques and mass communication and becomes more of a natural expression of the shared life that individuals have discovered in the cell group.

Howard Snyder argued that modern evangelism has become too professional and, hence, impersonal. One advantage of small home-cell groups is that they offer a structure in which *personal* communication of the gospel is made. In this context, evangelism is said to have even a greater impact than mass media programs because they reach people in a more authentically warm, face-to-face manner.

Christian communication suffers from impersonality. Often it is too slick, too professional, and therefore, too impersonal. But in a small group, person meets person; communication takes place at the personal level. This is why, contradictory as it may seem, a small group may really reach more people than the mass communication media. The mass media may reach millions superficially but few profoundly. . . .

The evangelism which will be most effective in the city will use small groups as its basic methodology. It will find the small group provides the best environment in which sinners can hear the convicting, winning voice of the Holy Spirit and come alive spiritually through faith. It will find that faith is contagious when fellowship is genuine.[32]

Home cell groups are designed to train all believers to be lay ministers and function in their fullest capacity within the body of Christ. Each person is expected to discover and develop his or her spiritual gifts, as described in 1 Corinthians 14, and to use them in service to strengthen the body. This is a dynamic concept of the church as a fluid collectivity (rather than as a static institution) in which all members have something to offer through their spiritual gifts as a contribution to the greater whole. The role of spiritual gifts in strengthening mutual responsibility and community is imperative according to David Mains because, among other things, it produces an interdependence among its members.

> Every true member of the local church has a minimum of one gift, and most people have many. Since no one has every gift, and everyone has at least one, there exists an interdependence among the members of the church. Scripture teaches (1 Cor. 12:22-25) that the less spectacular gifts are more necessary than the showy ones. In other words, the church can go a long time without a miracle, but let it try to exist without acts of mercy or contributions! . . . How disabled the body of Christ has become because our primary purpose for church attendence has been to hear one man exercise his gifts, rather than to prepare all the people to develop their gifts for ministry, not only within the church but also to society.[33]

Home cell groups differ organizationally from the house groups previously discussed on the basis of leadership structure. Home cell groups are led by house group pastors.[34] As mentioned earlier, this has certain implications for the organizational dynamics of home cell groups. Cell group leaders assume pastoral responsibilities for the members of their particular group. With home cell groups, we introduce the idea of multiple pastors who are approved by, and responsible to, a senior pastor of the local church. Leadership responsibilities and authority are delegated. Cell group members relate to the group leader as a pastor, according to Cho.

> The cell leader becomes a kind of pastor to [the individual], although one who is responsible to the church. The cell leader knows each of the members of his group and can relate personally to their joys and problems with a kind of familiarity that a senior pastor cannot develop.[35]

The role of the senior pastor tends to shift toward being a pastor to underpastors. The senior pastor's role is more indirect with regard to the local church body: he takes care of the underpastors, and the house church leaders pastor the flock. The advantage of such a structure is that even with large numbers, members can get very personal attention and nurture from a pastor through the small group. The personal time and attention one pastor can give to individuals within a congregation is directly proportional to the number of people he serves.

Cho observed from personal experience that a single pastor cannot sufficiently know and offer personal guidance to thousands of people. He gives an autobiographical account of how he suffered a collapse from mental exhaustion and fatigue in an effort to try and pastor twenty-four hundred people. The delegation of authority to house church leaders both relieves the senior pastor of an unbearable burden and provides a church structure more conducive to meeting the personal needs of individuals as they arise.

In Cho's model, only the house church pastors teach, and lessons are based on church-approved outlines. However, other members are encouraged to function in body ministry through their spiritual gifts. Members are also encouraged to pray for each other, particularly for the sick. The role of the house church pastor is to provide guidelines for spiritual growth and to promote involvement in the group.

Another implication of the organizational structure of home cell groups is the greater level of expectations and commitment from members. For example, Cho said that every church member is expected to be involved in a home cell group. These groups are not seen as secondary to church membership but, rather, integral to the effective operation and ministry of the local body. This is viewed as both an expectation and an opportunity.

> Home cell groups, . . . provide a real opportunity for people . . . to find meaningful involvement in the life of their church. Not everyone can be an elder or a deacon in a large church; not everyone can teach Sunday school or provide counseling. But with home cell groups there is an opportunity for everybody to become involved.[36]

Members of Cho's home cell groups are also expected to attend the meetings on a regular basis. Attendance is not taken lightly, and when a member is unexpectedly absent from a cell group meeting, the house church leader contacts the absentee person the following day to learn why. Members are *accountable* to their pastor and the cell group, and, in turn, the group assumes *responsibility* for the care and welfare of the individual. Cho likened this relationship to an extended-family system.

> Each home cell group is like a family circle. Through these family circles people feel a sense of belonging, and they are kept in the church. On top of that, each cell leader watches over his or her little flock, just as a hen watches over her chicks. He is constantly caring for the needs of his flock. But at the same time,

if one member of his cell group "plays hooky" from church, the following day the leader calls to find out if anything is wrong. If anything is, he can go and attend to it right away. Perhaps the person is ill or having some other problem that can be handled through prayer and ministry. And if he is really backsliding, the leader can determine the source of the problem and discuss it with him.[37]

Not all home cell groups, of course, are as tightly supervised as those described by Cho. However, these types of house groups do tend to exhibit greater expectations of their membership. Home cell groups tend to be characterized by organizational requisites such as consistent attendence, involvement in collective tasks or activities, and the acceptance of shared responsibilities for other members in the group. In the case of the latter, for example, members may help out other members in a variety of ways. Our research turned up numerous examples of persons who had lost jobs and were aided financially by the cell group. Repeatedly, we uncovered situations where women in a cell group had rotated responsibilities for cleaning house or preparing meals for a member family who was sick. We found that men in these groups often gave time on weekends to help others do certain tasks such as helping families move into a new house or paint an old one. Cho cited an instance where one cell group "even took up a collection to help send one of [their] family's children to college!"[38]

Earlier, in our discussion of home fellowship/share groups, we noted that the looser structure of such groups may contribute to an occasional inability to build commitment among members, thereby failing to realize primary group relations. In contrast, home cell groups are structured to require greater sacrifice of their members and therefore have greater potential for generating commitment and community (*koinonia*). Or to

7999 2

put it differently, they provide organizational structures which promote, prompt, and encourage the practice of love and sacrificial action in a concrete setting. In effect, the cell group becomes the real-life laboratory in which the mandates of Christ may be practically applied.

One additional comment about home cell groups seems worth mentioning. This concerns the overemphasis on group life which produces clannishness or exclusiveness. Several writers have warned against the "closed group" phenomenon which can occur in some situations. Howard Snyder suggested that churches employing small home-group meetings must keep in mind that they are only a means to a desired goal.

> The small group has been rediscovered as a structure for community life. I see this emphasis also as necessary and biblical. But an exaggerated emphasis here can produce an unhealthy, subjectivistic, pulse-taking kind of Christianity which is ingrown and fuzzy on doctrinal truth. Renewal and community are not ends in themselves.[39]

Snyder went on to say that small home groups must be evangelistic, open to growth, and in touch with the larger body of Christ. Again, the principle of cell division and growth seems critical here to help avert the problem of exclusiveness. Cell division is not always experienced as a pleasant plan of action for members who have developed deep relationships in the home group meetings.[40] However, the purpose of such action is designed to prevent the kind of exclusiveness and inwardness that can eventually undermine one of the most significant goals of cells groups—outreach and growth. The success of this model is largely dependent upon cell division and reproduction, or at least upon the willingness or openness to grow and divide.

Growth is inextricably tied to the assimilation of new persons into the small-group structure.

The Base-Satellite Unit

Base-satellite units include a variety of house church types which are sponsored by a host church. They may be distinguished from home cell groups in several ways. First, they are designed to operate with a greater degree of autonomy and self-sufficiency than home cell groups. They are semi-independent, and generally self-governing congregations which are often expected to become financially self-supporting.

This type of house church is more akin to the traditional concept of a mission. In the frontier Protestant tradition, many churches were begun in homes or makeshift facilities. The most significant departure from this idea is the deliberate intention to remain small and informal with the expressed purpose of attracting people who are uncomfortable in a formal, institutional church setting. In addition, these house groups differ from their counterparts in the past because they must function in an urban society.

An illustration of this model can be found in a study by David Chancey of churches in Fort Worth. The house churches that Chancey studied were referred to as "indigenous satellite units."[41] The term *indigenous* is meant to convey the idea of a ministry that is sensitive to, and compatible with, the the socioeconomic characteristics of the neighborhood or community. In the case of the Fort Worth study, the churches were located in working-class or blue-collar sections of the city. Other similar examples can be found in Louisville, Kentucky, Dallas, and many other Texas cities.

The informal atmosphere of a house church in a working class neighborhood is designed to break through some of the institutional trappings of middle-class religion that impede the effective communication of the gospel. As Snyder has correctly observed, traditional middle-class churches are often "a signpost telling the world of the church's class consciousness and exclusiveness."[42] The architecture or location of buildings can be a devastating witness to the church's pride, inflexibility, and class divisions. The latent effect of much of institutionalized religion in American society has been an increased estrangement of the lower classes.

Church historian H. Richard Niebuhr wrote:

> Whenever Christianity has become the religion of the fortunate and the cultured and has grown philosophical, abstract, formal, and ethically harmless in the process, the lower strata of society find themselves religiously expatriated by a faith which neither meets their psychological needs nor sets forth an appealing ethical ideal.[43]

The same principle applies to ethnic minority groups (for example, Hispanic, Black).

Too often churches erect insurmountable racial or cultural barriers that clothe the message in a narrowly defined white-Anglo perspective. The result is a markedly less effective proclamation of the faith among minority groups. On the other hand, the indigenous satellite unit goes to where the people live. It is flexible, informal, mobile, and able to meet people on their own territory without the cultural obstacles that characterize most churches.

Unlike home cell groups, base-satellite units do not draw their membership from the host church. They constitute separate congregations. Members are recruited from the community in which the house church is located. However, they are tied to the host church in several ways. For example, the sponsoring church may supply a house church pastor who is a paid staff person. This allows the work to progress without the economic hindrance or strain that many pastors of new churches face. In turn, some satellite groups help support the work of the host church once they are self-sufficient financially. Chancey reported that members' gifts, after local expenses, were given to the sponsoring church and to some other denominational ministries.[44]

According to Charles Olsen, some lines of communication and control between the host church and the satellite exist. But "the satellite members do *not* participate in the program activities of the [host] church, even corporate worship."[45] The base-satellite has its own congregational life and worship. One example involved the Druid Hills Presbyterian Church in Atlanta which sponsored a work among Cubans. The language barrier prevented full participation in the church's Sunday programs, so they were encouraged to meet in a house church with the support and oversight of the host church. The satellite model allowed the group to preserve their ethnic identity and worship in their native language.

In Chancey's study, the host church, Gambrell Street, reportedly had six house church pastors on staff (and now has eleven). Several of these were seminary students at Southwestern Baptist Theological Seminary in Fort Worth. The satellite units themselves were semi-independent in that they determined their own format and program. Thus, the seminarians had an opportunity, as house church leaders, to mesh theory and practice. The effective use of seminary students was apparently enhanced because of a greater willingness, on their part, to experiment with novel or nontraditional modes of worship. Moreover, the practical experience and training that resulted from the seminarians' work with blue-collar families was said to be invaluable for urban ministry.

Like home cell groups, base-satellite units adhere to the principle of cell division and reproduction. Larger than home cell groups, they may reach up to fifty persons before dividing.[46] They are more likely to meet in rented facilities than some other groups because of space limitations. However, the goal is not to build a large congregation and "move up" to a permanently owned building. The importance of cell division and retaining the small-group structure is paramount. In the cases we have observed, however, growth of the satellite ministry has come through adding new groups rather than through planned division.

Satellite groups differ from the previous groups we have examined in that they are not supplementary meetings. They are not midweek meetings which supplement a corporate worship meeting on Sunday. Though they may hold some meetings during the week, base-satellite units conduct church services in homes or rented houses on Sundays. They are alternative types of teaching/worship services. In a manner of speaking, they are "churches in homes," and probably invoke an idea which most people associate with the notion of house church.

The House Church

In keeping with everyday usage we have called the final type the house church. This type is totally independent and self-contained. It is not a satellite unit of an institutional church. Unlike a home cell group, it is not a subunit of a host church—though groups may be federated or voluntarily associated in other ways.[47]

Despite some differences, house churches share many common characteristics of home cell groups. Unlike home fellowship groups or home Bible studies, they are more tightly organized, and members generally do not attend other churches. They see their primary if not exclusive commitment to be the house church, and membership is more costly in terms of organizational requisites and expectations. Members are expected to make greater investments of their time, energy, and resources. In turn, they expect to reap greater rewards for their efforts.

The house church has a strong sense of affinity, harmony, and interconnectedness among its members. Generally, commitment may be described as total or undivided. It typically exceeds other types of house groups in its emphasis on group involvement, mutual responsibility for members, and the preservation of community. Indeed, among some groups, the emphasis on group commitment has been a source of conflict with regard to external family and friendship ties.[48]

There are two types of house churches: (1) autonomous, and (2) federated. Autonomous groups are formally unrelated to other similar-type groups or churches while federated groups form a cooperative association or community. However, these types may simply reflect different stages of growth. The autonomous house church may simply be at an earlier stage of maturation without the opportunity to form a second sister congregation. One cannot assume that the autonomous house church desires insulation from other groups. Research suggests otherwise. For example, the pastor of Jubilee Fellowship of Germantown, an autonomous house church in Philadelphia, states, "We are unhappy about the fact that we are an isolated congregation. . . ."[49] The church, which began as a home fellowship group of nine persons, has developed into an autonomous house church with a pastor and a membership of twenty adult members, nineteen children, and approximately thirteen others who attend regularly.[50] Jubilee Fellowship may express the sentiments of other autonomous house churches.

Isolation can be a development peculiar to the group's own history, and not a deliberate choice. Our research shows that either by arrangement or growth, an autonomous house church may develop into several related, but distinct, congregations thus becoming a federated type.

The second type of house church is the federated community. Federated communities constitute an aggregation of sister congregations. These are not to be confused with home cell groups. The basic distinction between home cells groups and federated house churches revolves around how they relate to other groups or churches. Cell groups exist as a program of a host church. The model is one of supplementary home meetings which are more conducive to adaptation by traditional churches. On the other hand, federated house church communities are independent collectivities which relate to each other by agreement. They typically arise outside institutional boundaries, though some may eventually attach themselves to a denomination.

With emphases on community and discipleship, these groups normally have stringent conditions for membership which test the intention and seriousness of each individual. For example, in Church of the Open Door, in San Francisco, individuals are expected to take an intensive twelve-week course covering the church's organization, doctrine, philosophy, direction, and goals as a condition to membership. Church of the Open Door, San Francisco, is a loose association of three separate congregations with their own pastors who meet primarily in small house groups but come together at regular times for corporate worship, prayer festivals, or joint ministry activities. Would-be members must also demonstrate their involvement in the church for a period of nine months before being admitted.

Church of the Open Door insists on having persons who are going to be active in the body.

Church of the Savior, in Washington, DC, is another example of a federated community. The church consists of "four, fully autonomous sister communities."[51] Persons seeking to become part of the church body must take five classes over a period of two years to qualify for membership. All members enter into a covenant, renewed annually, which commits them to daily prayer, daily Bible study, weekly worship, and tithing. House churches, referred to as mission groups, consist of five to twelve people who "share unlimited liability for one another."[52] Each member of a house group reports weekly on failures and successes of covenanted disciplines as well as sharing personal problems, needs, insights, and joys. Members also share some financial accountability for each other. Though not communal, needs are presented to the group for aid and assistance when the situation calls for collective action.

Still another example of a federated community is the Houston Covenant Church. As one of the many "covenant communities" or fellowships across the country, the Houston Covenant Church (HCC) asks every member to submit to the authority of a house church pastor or "shepherd" in order to achieve effective discipling of novitiates. The HCC is an "intentional community" built around small groups ("covenant fellowships") meeting in homes. The more than a dozen house groups in the HCC, each headed by a "shepherd," exist in a covenant relationship with each other and with the other groups as "fellow bond servants" in Christ. One requisite of membership in the church is the establishment of a servant-teacher relationship between disciple and shepherd that is designed to replicate Jesus' methodology of training His own disciples. Through this method, it is believed that members can be more thoroughly equipped to live a radical Christian life-style in a non-Christian culture.

Groups of this type tend to invoke the biblical imagery of "pilgrims" and "strangers" in an alien world (compare 1 Pet. 2:11; Heb. 11:14). This is a strong source of identity for the HCC. But the use of home meetings also has quite practical reasons for the group—it conserves economic resources, permits greater intimacy, and is more conducive to one-on-one discipling of members.

House churches make up distinct organizations that are part of the larger house group movement. But they are distinguished on the basis of their more comprehensive life-style and world view. House churches are more inclusive, more dynamic, and more engaging of members' time, energies, and resources than other types of house groups. Persons who join such groups seek to involve their whole lives in church and community. The compartmentalization of religious and secular activities tends to dissipate. Commitment and identification with the group is pervasive.

The following comments by a senior pastor of a covenant fellowship in South San Francisco (Covenant Outreach Ministries) convey the seriousness with which they see their calling.[53]

> We are a group of "covenant people." That means we believe God has divinely placed us in covenant responsibility to Him and with each other. Christianity is not "freedom," it is rather divine bondage. We are, as God reveals and confirms, bonded or covenanted one to another as to further God's goals and remove our fleshly natures as the challenges of covenant relationships lead us to our crosses.[54]

The intensity of commitment expressed here is not typical of what one finds in most institutional churches. It would appear that the house church is a vehicle for persons seeking greater levels of religious involvement. The idea of federated communities is not unlike that of the primitive church in the first century. Church historian Floyd Filson has argued that the early church was essentially built around a network of house church communities in the cities.[55] He also suggested that it was in these close-knit groups that the early church was able to survive in the face of a hostile culture. It may be argued, then, that it is not a coincidence that these types of groups should emerge in a social climate of pervasive secularism.

Beyond the Five Types

Some observers may suggest that additional types of house groups exist or may come to exist. They are probably correct. One type, which we did not cover because it is designed to be temporary, is the church-type mission which meets in a home. This is essentially a temporary house church. These have been used for centuries to start new work, but they are not considered in this book because there is no commitment to home worship and to the house church as a legitimate enduring form of church structure. Other house groups may fall between the categories or have emphases which strain our definitions. We recognize the problem, one which is shared by all typologies.

In the next two chapters, examples of two major types of house groups are described in detail: the home cell group and the house church. These types are singled out because they are the most controversial and are creating the most interest and enthusiasm. In each case two examples are presented, and in order to illustrate both positive and negative aspects of the movement, we have included groups that have experienced problems as well as successes.

Notes

1. Francis M. DuBose, "Alternative Church Models for an Urban Society," eds. Larry L. Rose and C. Kirk Hadaway *The Urban Challenge: Reaching America's Cities with the Gospel* (Nashville: Broadman Press, 1982), p. 141.

2. Lawrence O. Richards, *A New Face for the Church* (Grand Rapids: Zondervan, 1970). Paul Yonggi Cho with Harold Hostetler, *Successful Home Cell Groups* (Plainfield, N.J.: Logos International, 1981).

3. Robert C. Girard, *Brethren, Hang Loose* (Grand Rapids: Zondervan, 1972), p. 60.

4. Ralph Neighbour, *Touch of the Spirit* (Nashville: Broadman Press, 1972).

5. Philip Anderson and Phoebe Anderson, *The House Church* (Nashville: Abingdon, 1975).

6. DuBose, "Alternative Church Models for an Urban Society," p. 140.

7. David Chancey, "The House Church," *Missions USA*, Jan./Feb., pp. 57-58.

8. Charles Olsen, *The Base Church: Creating Community Through Multiple Forms* (Atlanta: Forum, 1973).

9. John Marx and Burkhart Holzner, "Ideological Primary Groups in Contemporary Cultural Movements," *Sociological Focus*, vol. 8, issue 4, pp. 311-329.

10. Ibid., p. 316.

11. See Girard, *Brethren, Hang Loose*, pp. 216-220, for partial reprint of *Lay Trainees Manual;* Jimmy Long, "Inductive Bible Study," *Small Group Leaders' Handbook* (Downers Grove, Ill.: Inter-varsity Press, 1982).

12. Cho, *Successful Home Cell Groups*, p. 49. See also George Webber, *God's Colony in Man's World* (Nashville: Abingdon, 1960) p. 27.

13. Anderson and Anderson, *The House Church*, pp. 7-8.

14. Charles H. Cooley, *Social Organization* (New York: Scribner's, 1962), p. 23.

15. Ibid., p. xviii.

16. Ibid., p. 33.

17. Girard, *Brethren, Hang Loose*, p. 146.

18. Cooley, *Social Organization*, p. xix.

19. Rosabeth Moss Kanter, *Commitment and Community* (Cambridge: Harvard University Press, 1973).

20. Neighbour, *Touch of the Spirit*, p. 89.

21. Lawrence O. Richards, "The Body of Christ: God's Setting for Learning the Bible," ed. Ralph Neighbour, *Future Church* (Nashville: Broadman Press, 1980).

22. Ibid., pp. 130-137.

23. Girard, *Brethren, Hang Loose*, p. 154.

24. Ibid., p. 135.

25. Ibid., p. 137.

26. Ibid., p. 146.

27. Ibid., p. 95.

28. Ibid., p. 149.

29. Ibid., p. 150.

30. Cho, *Successful Home Cell Groups*, p. 58.

31. Robert Raines, *New Life in the Church* (New York: Harper and Row, 1980, Revised and Updated Version), p. 59.

32. Howard A. Snyder, *The Problem of Wineskins: Church Structure in a Technological Age* (Downer's Grove, Ill.: Inter-varsity Press, 1976), pp. 141-142.

33. Quoted in Snyder, *The Problem of Wineskins*, p. 135.

34. See Roy Harthern, "Building the Body Through Fellowship Groups," *Charisma*, July-Aug. p. 39; Tommy Reid with Doug Brendel, *The Exploding Church* (Plainfield, N.J.: Logos International, 1979), pp. 130-131; Raines, *New Life for the Church*, pp. 86-88. Despite different names given to these groups, they are "cell groups" as we have defined them here.

35. Cho, *Successful Home Cell Groups*, p. 51.

36. Ibid., p. 50.

37. Ibid., p. 67.

38. Ibid., p. 53.

39. Snyder, *The Problem of Wineskins*, p. 17. For another discussion of potential problems and dangers see Oliver Powell, "The House Church and the Church System," ed. Arthur L. Foster, *The House Church Evolving* (Chicago: Exploration Press, 1976).

40. Cho, *Successful Home Cell Groups*, p. 66; Girard, *Brethren, Hang Loose*, p. 151.

41. Chancey, "The House Church," p. 57. This type is also quite similar to the "Satellite House Church" described by Olsen, *The Base Church.*

42. Snyder, *The Problem of Wineskins*, pp. 72-73.

43. H. Richard Niebuhr, *The Social Sources of Denominationalism* (New York: Meridian, 1929), pp. 31-32.

44. Chancey, "The House Church," p. 58.

45. Olsen, *The Base Church.* p. 81.

46. Ibid., p. 58.

47. DuBose, "Alternative Church Models for the Urban Church," p. 140.

48. See Bill Ligon with Robert Paul Lamb, *Discipleship: The Jesus View* (Plainfield, N.J.: Logos International, 1979); Bob Buess, *The Pendulum Swings* (Indianoloa, Ia.: Inspirational Marketing, 1974); Jerram Barrs, *Shepherds and Sheep: A Biblical View of Leading and Following* (Downers Grove, Ill.: Inter-varsity Press, 1983).

49. Artibus B. Sider, "Jubilee Fellowship of Germantown," ed. Ronald B. Sider, *Living More Simply: Biblical Principles and Practical Models* (Downers Grove, Ill.: Inter-varsity Press, 1980), p. 130.

50. Ibid., p. 125.

51. Ronald B. Sider, *Rich Christians in an Age of Hunger* (Downers Grove, Ill.: Inter-varsity Press, 1977), p. 198.

52. Gordon Cosby, *Handbook for Mission Groups* (Waco, Texas: Word, 1975), p. 63.

53. This church has since moved to Marin county and is now known as "Christ Church of Marin."

54. *Covenant Life,* 1979, p. 4.

55. Floyd Filson, "The Significance of Early House Churches," *Journal of Biblical Literature,* vol. 58, pp. 105-112.

5
The Home Cell Group

In this chapter, we present case studies of two churches which have made extensive use of home cell groups. They share many of the characteristics we have identified earlier, but they also represent a sharp contrast. One is affiliated with a denomination, the other is not. One has been influenced significantly by Cho's model while the other arose without any knowledge or awareness of this preexisting model. One church effectively integrated the cell ministry into its structure while the other was not able to do so.

The first case study, Elmbrook, represents a very successful and growing ministry of cell groups. It is an independent church which has pioneered new methods and training in this area, and we feel it one of the finest models in the United States.

The second case study, Hoffmantown, examines a church which had phenomenal success in only a few short years but ran into some problems with denominational traditions and attitudes in the congregation. We selected this second case because we feel it points out some of the issues and conflicts that denominational churches might face in organizing a home cell group ministry. It is not intended to discourage its use among such churches but to offer some understanding of the dynamics of organizational innovation and resistance to change. We could easily have selected one of the many other successful cases, but it is often equally helpful to learn why a group does not succeed.

Case Study One: Elmbrook Church, Milwaukee

History and Development

Elmbrook Church, Milwaukee, was founded in 1958, during a period in America which witnessed unprecedented levels of growth in church attendance and membership. Elmbrook Church benefited from this period in only a modest way. In the first twelve to thirteen years of the church's history, it saw a slow but steady growth. By 1970, Elmbrook had an average attendence of approximately three-hundred-fifty in Sunday morning worship services. In 1971, however, the church began to experience a large influx of members. Much of this was due to the Jesus movement and to the resurgence of interest in evangelical religion among certain groups of previously disaffected youth. From 1970 to 1972, the church grew in attendence from three-hundred fifty to about thirteen hundred. They were soon forced to move to an abandoned cinema to accommodate this extraordinary influx of young people. By 1974, the attendance was over two thousand, and the church had to relocate again.

In 1974, the church also began to examine some of the problems that this sudden growth had brought. The church found itself faced with a very different kind of challenge. They suddenly had a large number of people who had been in the church for only a short time and thus did not know each other. The church had grown numerically, but as one staff member put it, they had an "integration" problem.

Members were not being assimilated into the body, and they

lacked an awareness of being related to each other in love and commitment. This problem was accentuated by the oil crisis in the spring of that year which contributed to the escalating costs of gasoline and the increased difficulty of traveling across the city. Many of the members who were scattered around the metropolitan area were forced to reduce travel. Consequently, the church began to see falling rates of attendence at various meetings and functions. Though attendance on Sunday mornings remained stable, the development of an integrated community was suffering.

Sunday morning attendance was not enough. Church leaders felt that members could not exercise their spiritual gifts or realize genuine *koinonia* while sitting in a pew. These were activities more conducive to small groups.

In response to this dilemma, pastor Stuart Briscoe decided to initiate small-group ministries at Elmbrook. Briscoe made a careful study of small groups as they were employed throughout the Bible. He was particularly impressed by the parallel problem of rapid growth faced by the early church. Briscoe observed that the New Testament churches met from house to house and that "the Lord was adding to their number daily" in small groups or house churches (Acts 2:46). Rapid growth did not preclude assimilation of individuals into the local body of Christ. Curiously enough, pastor Briscoe proposed the use of home cell groups without any knowledge or awareness of the success Cho was having in Korea.

Before proceeding with the formation of home groups, the church conducted a study of groups already functioning in some capacity (home Bible studies, informal discussion groups) to avoid duplicating existing ministries. The church recognized a need for diverse groups, and these were encouraged to continue. But the purpose of the home cell groups, called Neighborhood Home Groups (NHGs), was to be more comprehensive than the other types that had already formed. Neighborhood Home Groups were designed to meet a broad range of needs within the body, including increased pastoral care and supervision and the nurture of relations among believers. Three reasons for these groups were cited by the church.[1]

(1) For developing a sense of community
(2) For assigning local responsibility
(3) For adequate overseeing

In the fall of 1974, the church began with ten Neighborhood Home Groups. These were in strategic geographical locations compatible with areas where members were concentrated. The groups averaged between twelve and fifteen persons in size. Each group was assigned a leader who was approved by a pastoral coordinator. In the initial phase, the groups were given a series of cassette tapes made by Briscoe and a set of study questions to promote discussion. At the conclusion of this series, the home groups were free to select their own topics and materials for future study.

In 1976, the church decided to form a task force to study ways of improving the quality of NHGs. The task force was comprised of one representative (the leader) from each of the groups. This effort was also a way of training leaders to become better facilitators of the home groups. Upon recommendation by the task force, a leadership enrichment program was instituted as a training format for all leaders of NHGs. This included (1) two quarters of Neighborhood Group leadership classes on Sunday mornings as a part of the adult Christian education program; (2) input from a summer intern; (3) an all-day seminar on leadership taught by a faculty member of Trinity Evangelical Seminary; (4) the establishment of a resource center and

library of tapes, books, and other pertinent study materials; and
(5) the formation of regular Leadership Enrichment Growth
Seminars (LEGS) to help leaders discover and deploy spiritual
gifts within a group and to help them understand the dynamics
of growth.

As the vision for these groups evolved, so did their effectiveness and maturity. To the credit of Briscoe, the NHG ministry
was not seen simply as an appendage or a temporary fad. It was
seen as a integral part of the church, to be cultivated with great
care and supervision. As a result, Elmbrook has become an
important and highly visible witness in metropolitan Milwaukee.

Organization

Elmbrook's Neighborhood Home Group ministry now en-
compasses fifty-nine groups and approximately eleven-hundred
persons. There are about ten groups which average between
twenty and twenty-five members, but the majority of NHGs
average about fifteen in size. The groups are divided into eight
distinct geographical regions. The purpose of regional divisions
is to establish a means of defining boundaries for localized
ministry and to identify areas for supervision by regional shepherds. It also provides a basis for monthly regional meetings of
NHG leaders. In these regional meetings, individual NHG
leaders are given the opportunity to get feedback from others
who have similar duties and responsibilities. Successes and failures are shared in an ongoing effort to increase the effectiveness
of house groups. Leaders also receive encouragement and edifi-
cation from their peers and the regional shepherd.

Above the regional shepherd is a pastoral staff member who
is employed by the church to oversee the NHGs on a full-time
basis. The church first employed an associate pastor for this

purpose in 1978 because of the overwhelming number of responsibilities and needs that arose in connection with the NHG ministry. The creation of this position has proved to be most fruitful. The home groups have flourished under the two persons who have occupied this position since 1978, Michael Frans and David Seemuth.

Among the duties of the senior coordinator of the NHGs is a regular schedule of visiting the groups to monitor progress, evaluate effectiveness, and suggest ways in which the groups may be improved. Each pastoral visit is accompanied by a follow-up letter to encourage the groups and their leaders. In the evaluation process, a diagnostic tool has been developed to aid systematic examination of means and goals. NHG leaders are provided copies for self-evaluation as well. It is the senior coordinator's task to make sure the groups have a clear understanding of their goals or intended functions.

To avoid having the groups regress to home Bible studies or discussion groups, the church has identified some very specific expectations of NHGs. The following list outlines these expectations.[2]

(1) *Nurture*—care and feeding of believers. Involves commitment to each other for mutual growth.

(2) *Visitation*—of new members, families, and friends.

(3) *Hospitality*—(Greek is *philoxenia,* lit. "love of strangers), use of home, greeting one another, preparing/ serving refreshments).

(4) *Follow-up*—specifically, new members.

(5) *Localized projects*—(nursing homes, reformatories, prison ministries, resettling refugees).

(6) *Discovery and coordination of transportation needs* —(for example, students, elderly, anyone in need).

(7) *Intergroup activities*—potluck dinners, picnics, and fellowship.

The formation of new groups operates on the basis of cell division and reproduction, as described in chapter 4. When an NHG grows too large, the leader may suggest forming another group with a nucleus of people from the original. The creation of a new group requires participation by the NHG leader and the group members in an initial orientation and must be approved by the pastoral coordinator. Approval of new groups is given when the following requirements are met.[3]

(1) The group understands and agrees to the overall purposes and functions of NHGs after initial orientation.

(2) The group agrees to being subject to Elmbrook's constitution policies and statement of faith.

(3) The group demonstrates after a minimal six-week period evidence that it is pursuing the purposes and functions of NHG life.

(4) The group agrees to participate in a periodic renewal for the purpose of reexamining its purposes and functions and evaluating its progress.

The Neighborhood Home Groups are designed to replace traditional midweek services at the church and any of the activities formerly within their domain. Here the church's commitment to NHGs is demonstrated further. No competing services or activities are offered at the church. Members are encouraged to attend NHGs and to become involved in a personal way in the lives of other believers. Brochures are distributed by the church describing the goals and activities of the home groups. A biweekly newsletter, *In Touch,* is also produced to inspire and inform interested persons about the needs and opportunities of neighborhood groups. Even a map is supplied showing the locations of NHGs and their members. Classes are offered on a continuing basis through the Christian education elective program on Sundays designed to define and clarify the purpose of NHGs. The NHG ministry is an important part of the church, not just an ancillary program for the youth.

Those involved in NHGs represent all age groups. According to David Seemuth, the current pastoral coordinator of the NHG ministry, the church encourages participation from all age levels. The largest age division, however, is young marrieds and singles, aged twenty-five to thirty-five. This is to be expected since, proportionately, they are also the largest age group in the church. It may be noted that the church does operate some interest groups which are comprised exclusively of young marrieds and singles, but these are not substitutes for NHGs. One of the initial purposes for starting neighborhood groups was to integrate members, of all ages, into the church body. Pastor Seemuth sees this as an important focus to be cultivated and maintained. One of the challenges he faces is to persuade young singles to expand their small circle of relationships to include marrieds and older members in the church. He makes the following comments about assimilating singles into the Neighborhood groups.

> The Neighborhood groups are comprised of people of all ages and marital statuses. . . . I think for singles, though they may not feel they need families around, you know, because they love to associate with (other) singles, they also need that kind of relationship with older people and with people who have families that are established. I think it is good for their emotional health.[4]

Becoming involved in the lives of people dissimilar from

oneself is believed to be part of the maturation process. It exposes one to the needs and emotions of people with different backgrounds or at different phases of the life cycle.

One of the most commonly asked questions about house church groups is: What do you do with the children? Elmbrook's policy on this matter is to allow each NHG to determine its own arrangement based on the needs of the group members. As might be suspected, there are many different kinds of arrangements within the total configuration of NHGs.

Some groups rotate responsibilities for supervising the children. One person or couple is assigned to take the children each week until all members of the group have participated, and the rotation begins again. In a typical group, this means one would have responsibility for the children about once every six to eight weeks. In a similar manner of rotation, some groups arrange to leave the children at a different member's home, forming a type of co-op. A few of the groups allow the children to remain in the meeting. Other groups have opted to hire baby-sitters, especially when the children are very young. Still others have made arrangements to leave the children at home with a friend or baby-sitter.

The agenda of a Neighborhood Home Group meeting follows the general guidelines established by the pastoral coordinator. Meetings are usually held on Wednesday evenings and begin at seven o'clock. They typically last about two hours. As people arrive at the home of the host family, they are greeted at the door by the group leaders. Following a brief period of exchanging names and indulging in some casual conversation, the group is asked to be seated, and the home group leader formally recognizes the visitors.

To facilitate an atmosphere of openness and acceptance, the leader asks each individual in the room to introduce himself or herself and adds, "Please give us a word which describes how you feel tonight." As persons describe their feelings or current state of mind, people are drawn into the group, and one can sense the psychological barriers dissipate. By the time the introductions have been made clockwise around the room and reach the visitor, one already feels a part of the small group and experiences a sense of familiarity with the members.

From this initial phase of the NHG meeting, the group is led into a time of worship and singing. One of the members plays a guitar, and the leader encourages everyone to concentrate on worshiping the Lord, putting all distractions aside. Members enthusiastically express their praise to God. Songs or choruses which the members know by heart are also introduced spontaneously during this period of unstructured worship. One of the choruses is from Psalm 35. The leader stops, reads several Scriptures, and then suggests that the group do some of the things contained in the passage. The group responds by showing greater concentration and enthusiasm in their worship. This period of the meeting lasts about twenty minutes.

The group then turns to a time of Bible study. The leader assigns three persons to read preselected verses from the New Testament. After these are read aloud, he examines them exegetically and then opens the lesson up for group discussion. Those who have something to contribute are encouraged to speak. Approximately forty-five minutes of the meeting is spent in Bible study. Following this, the leader takes prayer requests and asks the group to remember each of them as they proceed into a conversational prayer format. The prayer time ends after about fifteen minutes, and then the group is invited to stay for fellowship and refreshments. Overall, it is an atmosphere in which anyone could feel comfortable while hearing the gospel and observing the body of Christ in worship.

The operation and organization of these cell groups reflect ten years of planning and work. Many hours have been invested in the NHG concept, and their work has paid off. Elmbrook may have the most advanced model of home cell groups in the country.[5] Policies and guidelines have been delineated in almost every area of operation. Their handbook is, by far, the most complete we have seen. It includes planning reports, evaluation worksheets, diagnostic instruments, profile forms for NHG members, a directory of NHG leaders and members, leadership training materials, a statement of policies and procedures, and a bibliography of small groups. Churches interested in developing or improving a home cell group ministry could benefit greatly from this model.

Authority Structure and Beliefs

Despite Elmbrook's size, the NHG model provides an authority structure which can give adequate pastoral care and nurture to hundreds of persons in small, intimate settings. One of the keys to the success of NHGs is the effective organization and development of leadership. Responsibilities for supervision exist at multiple levels, making the operation of NHGs more manageable and placing leaders in clearly defined roles of service and accountability. Every NHG member is supervised by his or her leader; every leader is supervised by a regional shepherd; the regional shepherds are under the charge of the pastoral coordinator; and the pastoral coordinator reports to the senior pastor. Figure 1 gives a graphic illustration of how the NHG ministry is structured.[6]

The qualifications for NHG leaders are taken from I Timothy 3 and Titus 1:6-8. The church has gleaned a number of criteria from these passages, and they are applied to persons desiring to be a NHG leader. All NHG leaders must be mem-

Figure 1

Organizational Structure of Authority/Leadership
of Elmbrook's Neighborhood Home Groups (NHGs)

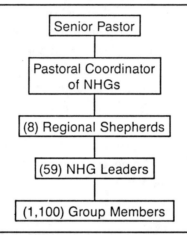

bers of Elmbrook, and, in most circumstances, they are expected to have been a vital part of an existing NHG. Potential leaders typically become part of what is called a "core group" if they are serious about becoming a leader.

A core group consists of two couples or one couple plus another individual who are firmly committed to the ongoing life of the NHG. They serve as a support group for the leader and help share the load and privilege of ministry. The leader knows that these people can be relied upon to assume various tasks and duties when asked. The purpose of instituting core groups is to promote ownership of the vision and functions of NHGs and to prevent leader burnout.

The guidelines for the training of Neighborhood Home Group leaders have been developed systematically and are graphically illustrated in Figure 2.[7] The complete training of a leader (from member to regional shepherd) is said to involve eight distinct phases. In phases 1 and 2, potential leaders are identified and given opportunities to lead the group, particularly if the normal NHG leader is away. In phase 3, the potential leader is invited to a NHG Leadership Training Class, held quarterly. If completed satisfactorily, the potential leader in phase 4 is then interviewed by the pastoral coordinator, to determine the individual's intentions and qualifications. In phase 5, the potential leader participates in thirteen weeks of one-to-one study with the pastoral coordinator on the general subjects of Christian life and leadership. In phase 6, the individual who successfully completes the course is given responsibilities for a NHG, upon recommendation and approval by the pastoral coordinator and the regional shepherd. Continual training for the NHG leader is provided in regional meetings,

Figure 2

Phases of Training for NHG Leaders
(From Member to Shepherd)

L M M M M M M M M M M *M* M	**PHASE 1**—As a member (*M*) of NHG who demonstrated faithfulness, responsibilities are given by leader. Person or persons will probably be part of core group.
L M M M M M M M M M M *M* M	**PHASE 2**—Member (*M*) has shown responsibility at phase 1 and has real potential as leader. *M* may be asked to lead the group if leader needs to be away.
PC *M M M M M M** M M M M M M	**PHASE 3**—Member (*M**) is invited by leader to NHG Leadership Training Class held quarterly for all from phase 2.

Attendence does not commit one to become a leader.

M*---›PC   *PHASE 4*—After phase 3, interview with potential leader (M*) is conducted by pastoral coordinator to determine desires and qualifications for NHG leadership.

L----›PC   *PHASE 5*—Person (L) is qualified and desires to become leader. He then undergoes thirteen weeks of one-to-one training on Christian life and leadership with PC.

        L   *PHASE 6*—New leader now has own
M *M* M M M M   NHG and begins to delegate responsibili-
M M M M M M   ty, forming core group, and so forth.

      RS   *PHASE 7*—Training for leader contin-
L L L L L L   ues. Three times a year, leader must at-
L L L L L L   tend Regional Meeting conducted by Regional Shepherd.

RS---›PC   *PHASE 8*—Exceptional leader may be promoted to Regional Shepherd who works very closely with pastoral coordinator.

in phase 7. Phase 8 is reserved for exceptional leaders who may be promoted to regional shepherd.

This phase-graded system of leadership training reflects a very sophisticated psychological understanding of how such skills are identified and developed. One can see the careful planning and attention that has been invested in NHGs to insure and perpetuate quality leadership. Elmbrook has constructed a framework by which individuals with the proper qualities or gifts can emerge and mature as leaders. The entire system is designed to encourage persons with such propensities by offering them invaluable guidance and practical experience. In this backdrop, it is not difficult to understand why Elmbrook has had an effective home cell group ministry.

The concept of NHGs is a logical extension of Elmbrook's approach to ministry in the city. The church is held to be "a shared commitment to God's people." They frequently cite Jesus' command that we love one another as He loved us, thereby demonstrating that we are His disciples (John 13:34-35). The NHG is a way of practicing such a command in a face-to-face manner, with people whom we know. It translates the abstractions of love and discipleship to concrete situations. Individuals are given opportunities to serve and to minister in small groups. If the church is to be a "body" or a "family," there must be a commitment to relationships so that the reality behind these metaphors may be realized. David Seemuth, the pastor coordinator, sees the need to build relationships as imperative to the success of Neighborhood Home Groups.

> I often recommend, in the beginning, when a group is just starting, to concentrate on studying commands in the scripture that increase the *interaction* with one another. Because I think that as the groups begin, they need to really put a lot of emphasis on getting to know one another. If people don't have that, they usually do not have deep or lasting relationships. They have to build a good foundation on relationships.[8]

The church also believes that the NHGs are a means of "equipping the saints" for service and helping them to find and develop their spiritual gifts. Leaders are provided with a complete listing of the spiritual gifts and their biblical references in the NHG manual. Each of the gifts is defined and discussed. Leaders are also offered practical suggestions for discovering spiritual gifts in the group, and they are encouraged to spend time in group study on the subject. A bibliography of relevant books for study guides is provided. Elmbrook feels the groups should be the training ground for discovery and deployment of spiritual gifts. In the small group, the gifts can be awakened and their use disciplined. The proper and disciplined exercise of spiritual gifts produces unity so the church may be edified (1 Cor. 14:5).

Elmbrook is clearly on the cutting edge of the house group movement in the US. It has pioneered new areas of organization and developed techniques and materials which far exceed those of most other churches. In large part, this is due to the ten years of experience on which they have had to build. But it is also attributable to the foresight and capability of Stuart Briscoe. From the outset, he saw the larger purpose of small groups and attempted to design some structural safeguards in order to insure their stability and longevity. He also invested money and resources in the NHG ministry, not the least of which was selecting a full-time pastoral coordinator to oversee the groups. This arrangement has proved to be very effective and may be a helpful model for other churches with less experience in house group ministries.

The emergence of house group networks like Elmbrook's Neighborhood Home Groups signals a new day in urban church ministry. One could say that this is only the proverbial tip of the iceberg. Perhaps ten to fifteen years ago, these groups could have been dismissed as a passing fad influenced by the rise of the counterculture and its religious counterpart, the Jesus movement. But the generation of youth who entered the church during this period are now becoming integrated pillars of the church community. And they appear to have brought a sincere conviction with them—that the absence of intimate fellowship and genuine *koinonia* has impoverished the urban church.

The emerging forms of house churches and home cell groups are more sophisticated and better planned than anything we saw in the early seventies. Like the people who populated them, these forms have been assimilated by the church, and they have been transformed into effective vehicles of growth, nurture and evangelism.

Case Study Two: Hoffmantown Baptist, Albuquerque

History and Development

Hoffmantown Baptist began as a Southern Baptist mission in Albuquerque in 1954. The city was considered somewhat of an outpost by many and did not experience rapid urbanization until the 1960s. The church claimed about three-hundred-fifty members by the end of the first year. In the next twenty-three years, it would have four different pastors and approximately double in size. The first year of the current senior pastor, Norm Boshoff, was 1977.

Under Boshoff, Hoffmantown witnessed considerable growth. He is a dynamic, energetic person who began to introduce a number of changes in the church. One of the changes included adding new staff members to generate community interest, attract new members, and expand the ministries of the church. Among the new staff members hired was Steve Kunkle, a graduate of the University of Oklahoma who had worked with Navigators and Campus Crusade ministries. He was given the position of minister of discipleship in 1979.

The following year, several members of the staff, including

Boshoff and Kunkle, attended a seminar held by Pastor Cho on home cell groups in Fort Worth. After hearing Cho, they became fascinated with the concept and began discussing possibilities of engineering cell groups at Hoffmantown. In April, 1981, these two men decided to travel to Seoul, Korea, for a firsthand look at Cho's home cell groups. They were impressed by what they saw. The church had generated thousands of cell groups throughout the city and was adding new groups at a phenomenal rate. There was nothing particularly revolutionary about the meetings themselves, they observed. The format was simple and could be enacted anywhere.

The two returned to Albuquerque the next week determined to implement a full program of home cell groups at Hoffmantown. Steve Kunkle was given the duties of pastoral coordinator of the cell groups. Between April and September of that year, he worked on designing the operation and organization of the cell group ministry. Simultaneously, the idea was given a major emphasis by the senior pastor. Boshoff intended to make a radical shift in the traditional Sunday School program with the idea that cell groups could provide the functions of discipleship and outreach. Sunday School would be teaching oriented or instructional.

In September, 1981, the home cell group ministry was launched. The groups were called Neighborhood Groups (NGs). They began with only a few, but the plan was to emphasize growth and reproduction. And grow they did. By October of 1983, just two years later, they had approximately eighty-five Neighborhood Groups, involving between six- and eight-hundred persons a week. It appeared that the NGs had unlimited potential for growth. However, during this same time, attendance at corporate worship services began to decline. There were several reasons for this decline including feedback from some members, particularly the older ones, that too much emphasis was being given to the Neighborhood Groups. As a result, the church withdrew its emphasis on the Neighborhood Groups and retreated to a more traditional church format stressing Sunday School.

Steve Kunkle was pulled out of the NG ministry and reassigned to oversee Sunday School. All but one of the regional overseers of NGs were also taken out and given different duties. In effect, the organizational support structure for the NGs was dismantled. The groups were told to continue if they desired, but the church's emphasis was shifting away from the NGs. By January of 1984, the number of NGs had dropped to fifty-five, and the projected number of permanent groups by the end of the decline was estimated at thirty. One must inevitably ask, "What happened?" Why did the Neighborhood Groups conflict with the overall growth of the church, and what contributed to their demise?

The factors that contribute to a situation such as this can be very complex and even peculiar to an isolated case. But the problems that arose in the case of Hoffmantown are probably not unique. There are some indicators to suggest typical problems when organizational innovation is both sudden and substantial. The problem is compounded when the organization is a traditionally religious one. We want to offer three possible explanations for the Hoffmantown case: (1) The implementation of home cell groups was too much, too soon; (2) the church failed effectively to define and communicate to its members the new role of the Sunday School within the proposed organizational change; and (3) the over-forty population of the church never felt ownership of the idea, nor were they effectively assimilated into the groups.

Organization

In terms of a strict organizational structure, Hoffmantown's Neighborhood Groups did not differ significantly from Elmbrook's NHGs. Though perhaps smaller in size, usually averaging between eight and ten persons, the NGs were quite similar in constitution. The groups were divided into five geographical regions. Like Elmbrook, the purpose of regional divisions was to identify localized areas in order to provide better supervision and pastoral care of the groups. Regional supervisors from the church staff were assigned to each district. Monthly meetings were held for NG leaders and led by regional pastors.

From the initiation of NGs, a full-time pastoral coordinator was assigned to them. The pastoral coordinator's duties were to provide input for the groups, help train and give direction to leaders, monitor their effectiveness, and supervise the overall operation of the NG ministry. Even weekly attendance records were kept and tabulated, and a breakdown of attendence by groups was given in the church's weekly newsletter. Groups which averaged twelve or more persons a week were encouraged to divide and reproduce. The pastoral coordinator helped facilitate numerous new groups and apparently with much success.

Another feature, similar to Elmbrook, was Hoffmantown's promotion of Neighborhood Groups through brochures and information packets. Though not as well developed or systematic as Elmbrook's, the materials distributed by Hoffmantown indicated a sincere commitment to the NGs. The most widely distributed brochure on NGs emphasized care, acceptance, love, and friendship building as benefits of involvement. The reader was encouraged to join a Neighborhood Group for "fellowship and nurture." A description of the purposes of NGs was followed by a plea from the senior pastor that "every member of Hoffmantown" belong to a neighborhood group.

One prominent feature of the NGs, however, was the underrepresentation of older members. In fact, very few adults over forty years of age could be found in the Neighborhood Groups. The overwhelming majority of participants were young married and singles. Of course, this is a characteristic of home cell groups across the country. But in a typical Southern Baptist church, the age distribution will probably represent a wider range of people than in many younger evangelical and charismatic churches employing cell groups.

It seems clear now that the over-forty age group was not comfortable with the idea of cell groups. The church had already seen a number of changes, and the introduction of home cells may have appeared as an effort to capitalize on a popular trend or fad. While tolerant of the idea as an attraction for youth, they probably did not foresee the full-blown explosion of cell groups, nor did they sincerely believe it would make a fundamental change in the direction of the church. The lack of participation on the part of this group suggests they did not feel ownership of the new program. This is a critical aspect of the problem since persons over forty generally have more power in the church and contribute disproportionately to the church budget. It also reflects a problem of confronting tradition when organizational innovation is introduced. Steve Kunkle, pastoral coordinator of the Neighborhood Groups, made the following observation.

> The reason the Neighborhood Group ministry will attract more younger couples and younger singles is because they're more open to new ideas, and the cells are a new idea. What we found (also) . . . was that it's the length (of time) in the body of Christ. People who are newer to Christianity and to the

Church love it. People who are rooted in the old way, and already have established ministries of their own tended to stick with what they were doing.[9]

Part of the resistance to change, no doubt, was attributable to the unwillingness of some individuals to break with traditional methods of ministry. But perhaps a more important problem was the leadership's failure to define and communicate to this group the new role of the Sunday School within the framework of the proposed change.

It appears that many of these individuals believed that Neighborhood Groups and Sunday School were mutually exclusive programs. The existence of one implied the negation of the other. The stated intention of church leadership, however, was to give to each ministry different functions. Unfortunately, these guidelines and delineations were never effectively conveyed to the church, and many felt that the ultimate goal was to phase out Sunday School. As a result, those church members who saw great value in the Sunday School program felt threatened. The pastoral coordinator admits that the church made some mistakes in this regard.

> Many people in our church, because of the heavy emphasis on the Neighborhood Group concept or the cell concept, people who were really attached to doing ministry in a more traditional way, felt abandoned. And we made some mistakes in that area. . . . I think at our church (the Neighborhood Groups and the Sunday School) became competitive because where we failed was effectively communicating to the body how the two could fit together. . . . What we did is, we said, "We're going with Neighborhood Groups," because we got convinced, and I'm still convinced, that the only way we are going to penetrate cities in our day will be through relational evangelism. Traditional methods will not accomplish the trick. We tried to communicate to our people that this was the key way to do it if we were going

to fulfill the great commission as Christ commanded us to. But we failed to give Sunday School a vision of how they fit into that picture; they felt abandoned.[10]

It appears that within the framework of the new structure, the purpose of the Sunday School was to teach, train, and educate, as well as provide some peer fellowship. According to Kunkle, these goals were similar to the traditional function of Church Training in Southern Baptist churches. The Neighborhood Groups, on the other hand, were to furnish a means of evangelism, discipleship, and nurture. Pastoral functions could be carried out in the small groups. These were complementary functions not competing ones. It seemed to be a viable model for the future. "I think our main mistake," says Kunkle, "was communication, not philosophy." He remains convinced that home cells are the most effective means of urban evangelism and church growth.

Though communication was probably the most critical factor in the de-emphasis of Neighborhood Groups, it was not the only one. There appear to be several indicators that the NG program was moving too fast and perhaps in the wrong direction. The sheer explosion of home cells created its own brand of confusion. In general, the church was not prepared for this kind of sudden success. Besides the internal complications arising from managing the rapid growth of Neighborhood Groups, the church was also thrust into local and national attention within the denomination. The high visibility achieved by Hoffmantown was a source of both favorable and unfavorable vigilance. Locally, there were complaints that the NGs were impeding the planting of other churches in the area. Nationally, Hoffmantown was being hailed by denominational personnel as an example to be emulated. The visibility and attention showered upon Hoffmantown only accentuated the problem.

A second indicator was the publication of a small booklet entitled: *Family Multiplication Plan*. The booklet was poorly conceptualized and issued prematurely. Under the family multiplication plan, groups were to be propagated in a fashion in which the orginator of the NG was the benefactor. Persons fortunate enough to see the number of groups reach thirty-two automatically became fully paid staff members. The insertion of this ill-advised plan inadvertently led to some intense competition among some members and subsequently was scrapped. Had more time and careful thought been given to the plan, most likely it never would have reached the publication stage. In short, the family multiplication plan was produced hurriedly and unreflectively.

A third indicator points back to the communication problem between the church leadership and the Sunday School. Training cell group leaders during the Sunday School hour clearly signaled which program was considered more important, and evidently very little was done to assure Sunday School leaders that the church staff was behind them.

All these factors converged to complicate further the task of building a cell group ministry at Hoffmantown.

Authority Structure and Beliefs

Hoffmantown constructed a logical authority structure and arrangement of leadership for its cell group model. The senior pastor retained ultimate responsibilities for the NGs. Under the senior pastor, the pastoral coordinator was the delegated administrative head and spiritual authority of the Neighborhood Groups. The pastoral coordinator worked directly with five regional pastors or supervisors. This group of leaders, three men and two women, met monthly with the coordinator to discuss problems and strategies and to offer each other mutual support and fellowship. Regional leaders functioned as pastors, according to Steve Kunkle, and were employed members of the pastoral staff.

Each of the Neighborhood Groups was assigned a cell leader. Standards for cell leaders were high. Cell leaders had to be members of the church and were required to complete a twelve-week training course called Basic Life-Style Ministry before they could be approved by a nominating committee. They were also expected to tithe to Hoffmantown and to demonstrate a willingness to work under the spiritual authority of the regional pastor.

In practice, NG leaders were taught to delegate responsibility to other members in the group. For example, they were urged to allow gifted individuals to teach Bible studies, prepare lessons, or lead in worship. In this manner, future NG leaders could be identified and discipled. Those who were believed to have potential for leadership were then encouraged to take the Basic Life-Style Ministry Course. NG leaders were also expected to move the group toward outreach and growth. NGs were required to reproduce at least one other group within the first year. They were also asked to show evidence of recruiting unsaved or unchurched persons. A standard of two converts, with baptisms, within the first six months was given the NGs.

The guidelines for promotion of Neighborhood Group leaders to regional pastors were specified in the following manner. After abandoning the family multiplication plan, there were four remaining qualifications which had to be met. (1) Regional pastors had to complete a series of Level 1 courses in a Bible School operated by the church (The Great Commission School). (2) They had to exhibit qualities of leadership as described in 1 Timothy 3:1-7; Titus 1:6-9; and 1 Peter 5:1-5. (3) Recommendations for promotion were needed from the pastoral coordinator, a personnel committee, and two thirds of the regional pastors. (4) Final approval had to be given by the senior pastor.

In terms of beliefs, Hoffmantown's Neighborhood Groups strongly reflected Southern Baptists' emphasis on evangelism. In fact, Steve Kunkle felt the major thrust of NGs should be evangelism. Nurture, fellowship, and community were believed to come spontaneously from the home cell meetings. The outward focus of ministry was said to enhance the spiritual growth of the groups and prevent them from becoming too exclusive or inwardly concentrated. He made these comments:

> Our view of *koinonia* was that if the group had an outward focus, then *koinonia* was a natural result. A group that is loving God and loving each other with a goal of winning the lost will see *koinonia* as a result. We saw that . . . the healthiest groups in fellowship were those that were winning people to Christ.[11]

Ironically, this perspective was gleaned from observations while visiting some of Cho's cell groups in Seoul. Hoffmantown's approach is actually a departure from Cho's model. It reverses the priorities of ministry. While Cho strongly advocates evangelism, he has argued that it is a logical by-product of a viable *koinonia* fellowship. For whatever reasons, Kunkle and Boshoff perceived things differently. It may be that such abstract goals or priorities are so intertwined that they cannot be isolated and treated independently in day-to-day life. Whether or not the effects of *koinonia* were producing evangelistic thrusts, or vice versa, would be impossible to say. We can only identify what Cho has said and what most other cell group ministries have emphasized.

It is possible that by concentrating on evangelism, as they did, they unintentionally contributed to the problem we have identified as too much, too soon. While growth is good in and of itself, it probably did not help the longevity of the Neighborhood Group ministry. Given the inadequate communication between the leadership and the Sunday School personnel and the subsequent resistance to change that arose, it would have been better had they grown at a slower rate. Certainly, the NG ministry would have appeared less imposing and less threatening to some members had their growth been gradual.

The Hoffmantown case suggests several strategies that traditional churches might want to consider in starting a cell group ministry. First, good communication is essential. An ongoing dialogue among church staff and the membership needs to be sustained in order to get feedback and allow effective monitoring of questions and apprehensions that will inevitably arise. A clarification of goals needs to be made so misunderstandings can be arrested and alleviated. This will make the laity more informed and less threatened. At the same time, clear communication at the early stages of cell group development may also bring some unanticipated obstacles to the attention of the leadership. It would be far more advantageous to build strategies with the knowledge of such obstacles (such as a clear role definition for Sunday School) than to operate in ignorance.

The second strategy is a corollary of the first. The church must feel ownership of the idea, and part of the challenge in accomplishing this task lies in effective communication. The church will not feel ownership if they do not have input into the design and implementation of cell groups. Not every suggestion has to be put into effect. It is the process of fielding suggestions that is perhaps as important as the substantive value of the ideas that come forth.

Members need to feel they helped give birth to the idea, that they helped shape and influence the constitution of this program or ministry. Not all members will participate in the home cells, but neither will they feel that the idea is a foreign concept imposed upon them from the outside. If they have a part in its development and implementation, they will be more likely to see it as their own, and it will be more likely to succeed with their support and participation.

A third strategy suggested by the Hoffmantown study is to be deliberate and not be rushed into a hasty construction of a cell group program. Many mistakes can be avoided by careful planning and evaluation of other effective models or ministries. We have already seen that while the cell groups seem like a very simple concept, they can be quite complex in structure and practice. In addition, there are numerous complications that can emerge when actions come before adequate preparation.

Finally, churches need not eliminate or relegate to insignificance programs which are highly valued by the laity and the larger denomination. The pastor of a Baptist church would be ill-advised to replace Sunday School with home cell groups. Similarly, pastors in other denominations must avoid the impression that the cell groups are replacing or supplanting anything that is valued or has the force of great tradition behind it. New churches and independent churches may be freer to experiment, but they too should avoid arbitrarily throwing out traditional programs.

Notes

1. Taken from a brief case study (p. 2) of Elmbrook by Michael Frans which appears in the *Neighborhood Group Leaders Manual.* The authors wish to thank Michael Frans for this helpful overview.
2. Ibid., p. 3.

3. *Neighborhood Group Leaders Manual,* (no copyright date given), see "Policies and Procedures" section. Unpublished.

4. Personal interview with David Seemuth.

5. With, perhaps, the exception of Full Gospel Tabernacle in Buffalo, N.Y. This church has nine district pastors and an intermediate level of district leaders between the pastors and the cell group leaders. For information about obtaining a copy of their handbook, write David Hernquist, Full Gospel Tabernacle, 3210 Southwestern Blvd., P. O. Box 590, Orchard Park, N.Y. 14127-0590.

6. This chart was developed by the authors based on interviews and material found in the *Neighborhood Group Leaders Manual.*

7. Adapted from a graph in *Neighborhood Group Leaders Manual.*

8. From interview with David Seemuth.

9. From interview with Steve Kunkle.

10. Ibid.

11. Ibid.

6
The House Church

In this chapter, we describe two examples of the house church in detail. These descriptions are not intended to be representative but merely illustrative of the range and variation found among house churches. We offer some comparative analysis between the two in order to illuminate the internal dynamics of their organizational structures and to evaluate prospects for practical application and/or modification.

Case Study One: Houston Covenant Church

History and Development

In the late 1960s, Charles Simpson, a well-known leader in the Charismatic movement, left his church in Mobile, Alabama, to join several other important figures (for example, Derek Prince, Don Basham, Bob Mumford) in a teaching ministry based in Fort Lauderdale, Florida. This teaching ministry, Christian Growth Ministries, became very influential as it grew in size and popularity through the late sixties and early seventies. Since the Charismatic movement had very little formal structure and certainly no formal leadership, this organization had high visibility. To many, they appeared to be a prophetic vanguard.

Several men in the church that Charles Simpson left in Mobile began to meet privately in homes during the early seventies. Responding to the intensity and enthusiasm of the teachings of Simpson and Christian Growth Ministries, these men attempted to establish and develop deep commitments and relationships based on what they had learned. These emerging ideas later solidified as the controversial concepts of "shepherding" and "discipleship."[1] Essentially, they proposed a more intense relationship between the pastor and the layperson, with the former taking a greater authoritative role.

Both the organization in which Simpson was involved and these laypersons from Mobile shared a growing dissatisfaction with traditional forms of church government. The prevalent forms were felt to be too loosely structured and, therefore, ineffective. In 1972, Simpson returned to Mobile to help implement the concept of discipleship using the vehicle of the house church. They immediately experienced overwhelming success; yet, precisely because of their sudden growth, they also experienced a number of unanticipated problems. One major problem they encountered was an insufficient supply of "shepherds" or pastors to take care of the incoming members. There was a strong feeling among this group, however, that lay leaders could be informally trained and developed as effective house church pastors. After all, they reasoned, this was how Jesus trained His disciples to become leaders.

In an effort to mesh theory and practice, and to get a broader input from others in the larger charismatic community, they held the first Shepherd's Conference in 1972. This would be only the first of three such conferences to be held, the last in 1976. The overall reaction from the larger charismatic community was mixed. Some people were concerned that this direction of ministry, emphasizing discipleship, would become preoccupied with lines of authority and, therefore, were reluctant to endorse it. However, this did not deter Simpson and others from pursuing their convictions and beliefs. Others were drawn to this emerging movement and expressed considerable enthusiasm.

Shepherds were typically recruited among younger Christian men who had no seminary training. Many were involved in the Jesus movement and thus were already noninstitutionally oriented. One such individual was Keith Curlee, the eventual leader of the Houston Covenant Church. Curlee left Baylor University in his third year to enter the ministry on a full-time basis. He subsequently spent two years on the road as an evangelist. Upon hearing Simpson on several occasions and becoming convinced of the validity of the ideas he was advocating, Curlee decided to submit himself to the rigors of what some were now calling the "shepherding movement."

After a period of approximately two years, Curlee also became a shepherd and began a ministry in Gautier, Mississippi. He acquired a small number of members, mostly young couples, over a period of about eighteen months. In 1977, he was commissioned by some of the elders of the movement to relocate to Houston and begin a work there.

Curlee brought his entire congregation with him to Houston. Members were apparently given a choice to stay and become involved with a similar group or to move. They reportedly chose to move. Part of the reason for selecting Houston was that Curlee's wife had grown up there. His wife's family was still in Houston, and Curlee had already developed numerous friendships in the city. These relationships provided a base from which to recruit new members. Most of the people attracted were between the ages of twenty and thirty and had been actively involved in the Jesus movement. Many were disappointed with the perceived stagnation of traditional churches.

Organization

The Houston Covenant Church is made up of a network of groups or "flocks" headed by house church pastors or shepherds. There are now thirteen full-time house church pastors, seven part-time pastors, and approximately four-hundred members in the HCC. Ideally, it is recommended that a house church leader assume responsibility for about twelve families, though sometimes more are included. A flock will typically number between twenty-five and thirty-five people, including children. The families are usually young married couples. Some have small children while others are childless.

There is a strong emphasis on families, child rearing, and family-centered activities within the HCC. Sex roles are traditional, with the father being defined as the head of the house. Only men are allowed to be pastors. Women do not take leadership roles except in ministry to other women. These women "ministers" are always wives of shepherds. Wives are encouraged to go to their husbands for spiritual counseling and guidance. Any spiritual direction or advice given to the family will go through the husband. Members of the HCC believe in a strict adherence to their view of the traditional family.

The house groups meet separately once a week in the home of the shepherd. They are typically closed meetings. Visitors or outsiders are rarely included. The rationale for closed meetings is that the time should be reserved exclusively for addressing the needs of the flock. It is not intended to be evangelistic. Rather, it is a time of body-oriented ministry directed at the "sheep" for whom the shepherd feels a deep responsibility and obligation. The HCC is insistent upon distinguishing between the role of "pastor" and "preacher." They contend that even the most conservative, evangelical seminaries design their course work to train and develop preachers, not pastors. Pastoring, they claim, involves a different set of skills and is oriented to believers. HCC's senior pastor explains:

> We began to redefine the word *pastor,* . . . The pastor is a shepherd. And what does a shepherd do? He tends the flock . . . [We] went back to the use of shepherding the flock of God. Peter says, "Shepherd the flock of God," and we kept using that word. Because "pastor" had been so misrepresented, that was like the other side of the pendulum, to call back that word to its [original] content, and what it meant.[2]

The agenda of the house church meeting has some unique elements though it is not altogether unlike some types discussed. The home meetings begin immediately with singing and worship. Much of the music is written by members of the HCC or sister churches in other cities and would be unfamiliar to most outsiders. The members are very expressive in their worship. Hands are raised; worship and praise is vocalized; some speak in tongues while others pray or sing in a more familiar manner. This period of worship typically lasts about half an hour. After this time, the shepherd may solicit prayer requests from the group. Each request is addressed individually, and the shepherd leads the group in prayer for the person making the request or for whomever the request is made. If the individual makes a request for himself or herself, he or she may be asked to stand. Members of the group then encircle the individual and lay on hands as they pray out loud. This part of the meeting is followed by teaching from the shepherd or possibly listening to a cassette tape of a recognized leader or elder in the movement. At the end of the teaching, members will respond by prayer or meditation. If the message is deemed especially relevant or pertinent to an individual's life situation, then the individual may ask for further prayer.

The tone of the meetings is very moving and absorbing, and distractions such as children are notably absent. The children are usually taken to one of the member's houses or kept in a separate room and supervised by younger, single women in the fellowship. If the children are kept in the same house in which the flock meeting is held, they may be asked to join the adults briefly for singing and worship. After that time, they are escorted to another room where they have separate activities, somewhat equivalent to Sunday School.

Since the meetings take place in the shepherd's home, it is both a church and a home. Consequently, the shepherd's home will be large enough to accommodate the small body of believers. Pastors in the HCC receive a supplemental housing allowance to purchase and maintain a house church. Their salaries are paid from a portion of tithes that go into an Elder's Fund. Tithing is expected of all members, unless extenuating circumstances can be shown. Salaries are proportional to the number of members in the flock and their respective incomes. Thus, tenured pastors who have older, more affluent members will receive higher salaries than younger pastors just starting out. However, these disparities do not appear to be significant since the HCC is still very young.

Once a month, all of the local groups meet jointly in one common facility. This facility is usually a rented building such as an elementary or junior high school auditorium. The meetings are held on Saturday evenings and are usually two to three hours in length. Unlike the small flock meetings, these larger celebration services are usually open to visitors. Members may bring friends or relatives. The thrust of the celebration service remains oriented toward the body. Visitors are invited to participate. But one does not get the impression that the agenda is significantly altered to accommodate outsiders.

The corporate worship is deeply moving and powerful. Worshipers are very expressive in their actions. They may clap, shout, jump, or even "dance in the Spirit." Again, the music may be unfamiliar to most persons. But, unlike the small meetings, words to the songs are provided by use of an overhead projector. Following an extensive period of worship and praise, which may last up to an hour, the senior pastor typically speaks to the church. The senior pastor is held in very high esteem. His words have a prophetic tone to them, and he speaks with absolute conviction. Indeed, the members of the HCC consider him to be a prophet of sorts. One follower remarked, "I believe he hears directly from God. If God is saying something today, then that's where I'm going to hear it." After the message is delivered, the senior pastor challenges the church to greater faith and servanthood. A prayer is voiced, God's blessings are invoked, and the believers walk away singing a song about the kingdom of God.

The corporate worship service is an important event. But it is not the primary vehicle of the HCC's ministry to the body. The small home groups are. This is evidenced by the fact that the HCC has deliberately avoided purchasing a building which would seat the entire congregation. Though they have had the funds to do so, they have opted instead to invest the money in areas of need and ministry to people. In the absence of construction expenditures and maintenance costs that normally go toward property, they have been able to salary thirteen pastors, provide them with suppementary housing allowances, and meet financial needs of members when they arise. As an example of meeting the financial needs of members, the HCC paid the salary of one member whose union was on strike for eight months. As a result of the HCC's actions, this member family was able to avoid an otherwise stressful period of economic hardship. The church paid the worker his full salary and the family experienced no loss of income. The HCC is quick to point to benefits such as these. Few churches of their size, they argue, could do what they have done.

Like many other young churches, the Houston Covenant Church began without any type of permanent facility. This was by design. They deliberately avoided using incoming funds to construct a church building. In one instance, where a pastor and his small congregation were absorbed by the HCC, a building that was owned by this small group was sold. The church building would have provided ample room for the entire HCC in 1978, but the expenses of upkeep were felt to be an unnecessary financial burden, particularly in lieu of the potential income that could be obtained from selling the property. They were in no hurry to build, and the church chose to sell the property and use the money in other ways.

The use of house churches is said to allow for developing and sustaining relationships at the most intimate level of interaction. They help create an environment more conducive to nurturing interpersonal warmth and care and a meaningful exchange of needs and concerns among the members. The principles underlying the use of house churches are propounded by the church's senior pastor in the following manner," "We felt like the foundations of solid relationships were more important than foundations made out of bricks and mud."[3]

Though the primary thrust of church organization is based on house churches, the group is not opposed to constructing buildings when it becomes economically feasible, and it offers a practical use of space. In 1982, they constructed an experimental building which houses the offices of all the pastors and also includes a meeting facility which will accommodate about one-hundred persons. The facility is used by the different congregations on a rotating basis and primarily functions as a means of periodic evangelistic outreach. This facility allows all of the individuals or families within a flock to invite guests, without the problem of overcrowding.

The experimental building was not constructed until approximately five years after they arrived in Houston—a fact which the leadership tried to emphasize. Their reason for waiting five years even to construct an experimental building was to insure a comfortable margin of adequate funds. The HCC wanted to reach a point at which the construction expenditures would not be a strain financially. The architectural design and most of the manual labor for the experimental building was supplied by members of the church, reducing building costs to a minimum. The church only paid to have the foundation for the building poured. All labor and construction beyond that was supplied by the membership.

Despite the disclaimer of wanting or needing bigger buildings, construction of any type of edifice is one step toward increasing institutionalization, and one must wonder if the HCC will not eventually gravitate toward more traditional patterns. At present, the church remains strongly committed to an alternative model of interlocking house churches. But a sustained effort will have to be made to preserve the unique network of small groups in their present form.

Authority Structure and Beliefs

The HCC places a great deal of emphasis on the concept of discipleship and, therefore, requires of its members a higher level of commitment than is normally expected or found in traditional churches. The degree to which the notions of submission and authority are stressed within the Houston church and its sister organizations in other cities has come under criticism by some religious leaders. The root of this criticism seems to be that such groups are largely independent of denominational supervision and are thus given to greater tendencies toward authoritarianism.[4]

The HCC, on the other hand, argues that it is attacking some of the most critical problems in the contemporary church: excessive individualism, the loss of spiritual authority, and the lack of church discipline. The HCC is a reaction to perceived inadequacies within existing forms of church government. According to this view, the modern church wields such little power or impact upon society because there is no effective authority structure to compel or require responsible actions of believers. Too much is left to individual whim or personal fortitude. Essentially, most churches today are ineffective because they are not really in touch with their congregations, and they make no demands upon their members. The HCC joins the cry of numerous other evangelical and fundamentalist leaders in declaring war against "secular humanism" and the "moral decline" of America.[5] For the HCC, the battle lines must be drawn around the organization of church government at the grass-roots level. This involves both the establishment of responsible spiritual authority and lay accountability within the local church.

During interviews with the HCC leader, we were told repeatedly that the term *kingdom* in the New Testament may be translated as *government.* The HCC sees their purpose or calling as helping to implement a government which requires moral accountability of its spiritual citizens. This authority structure places a greater emphasis on submission to recognized leaders or one's own pastor within the HCC. But how much authority is given to pastors? Where does one draw the line between too much authority and not enough? These are questions that will elicit no consensus among religious leaders. Nonetheless, the question of authority was posed to HCC's senior pastor.

Interviewer: How much authority does a pastor have?

Curlee: I would have to say he has as much authority as is submitted to him. Submission constitutes authority; authority does not constitute submission. In other words, I have no authority in anybody's life unless they give it to me. Submission is the act of giving authority to another person. I don't really have authority in any man's life except that which is given.

Interviewer: That's also impacted by the degree to which submission is encouraged. If people are taught to believe that submission is good, then there is that external constraint, so to speak, upon one submitting himself or herself.

Curlee: That's right. The question is "what" should be submitted, not just submission. Well, Ephesians 4 talks about the gifts, the fivefold ministries, and there is a difference between government and ministries, I think. In fact, the Charismatic Movement never sorted that out, because people came with personal prophecies, and that kind of thing, but they (imposed) their will; they forced it on people. That's governmental, when it should have been ministry oriented. If the prophecy goes out, and it is received, fine. But governmental is that criteria which a particular . . . church sets up that says, "To walk in this church, this kind of submission will be required." You can't get away without saying that. You don't have to put on paper that you have got peer pressure, you have got promotion, you've got all the things anybody else would have. The question is: How do you deal with it.[6]

The HCC has dealt with this question by making a claim to

legitimate spiritual authority in a governmental context. By implication, this means that individuals who join the church must be flexible and willing to comply with a certain level of expectations and demands. Under most circumstances, members of the HCC are obliged to abide by the spiritual directives of the leadership. In a reciprocal fashion, however, leaders are expected to demonstrate a foremost concern for their small congregations.

The HCC trains its members through a discipling method. Members submit themselves to a pastor/shepherd in a very serious manner. The commitment is not simply a verbal contract. It signifies a covenant between the pastor and the layperson. The pastor/shepherd covenants with the layperson to take a measure of responsibility for the individual's spiritual welfare. In turn, the layperson covenants to serve the pastor and the other members of the flock.

A mutual bond of obligation is forged which pulls members together in tight-knit community. Few relationships in the individual's life are believed to be as important. The covenant signifies a sacred relationship, and the HCC believes an individual has only three covenants: one with God, one with spouse, and one with the pastor and the flock. It is the bond of the covenant that gives the HCC its intense commitment and internal cohesion. To outsiders, such camaraderie appears overdone and even cliquish. To the members, the covenant relationship creates a place of comfort, hope, and shared commitment.

The leadership in the HCC feels a strong sense of accomplishment. They assume their responsibilities with deep conviction, and they also enjoy a special status within the group. Social relationships between shepherds and members are notably hierarchial. Leaders and members approximate the roles of master and disciple, respectively. Members/disciples commit themselves voluntarily but more or less completely. Members show considerable deference to their pastors and trust God to keep these leaders humble and nonexploitive.

One senses among the pastors that they struggle to achieve a balance between the humility and power their roles create for them. Still, most outsiders will tend to cringe at the idea of relinquishing such authority to one's pastor. Perhaps seeing oneself as a servant is not too difficult, but the thought of having a master is considerably more objectionable to most. The HCC, on the other hand, contends that both roles are necessary to reproduce a revolutionary body of believers reminiscent of the first-century church. HCC's senior pastor defends this controversial belief in the following statement.

> Luke 16 talks about the master and the servant, so with the disciple you have the (roles of the) teacher and the learner. But that's not a Western idea. When you read the word *disciple,* that's not teacher and student, there's a difference. The word *disciple* has connotations of master and servant—what we would westernize as teacher and class. [The master-servant relationship] has tremendous "governmental" force in a man's life; it shapes a person's life.[7]

It is the so-called Westernization or dilution of the discipleship model that the HCC contests. They defend their methods as more in line with those practiced by Jesus in the New Testament. The cultural context of Jesus' day, they add, was the Middle East, not the West. For the HCC, this has significant implications for church government. Young believers need to be trained and discipled by qualified pastors who will, in a covenant relationship, lay down their lives for the sheep. In turn, the sheep are faithfully to serve their pastors and the others who share the covenant.

In everyday life, this means that a large portion of one's time and energies go toward the needs and activities of the HCC. The collective interests or goals often take priority over individual interests. There is an exchange here that involves both costs and rewards.

It costs the individual more to belong to such a church because it will make more demands on his or her life. Members will be asked to participate in all the projects and activities of the church. Their lives will be more regulated, their attitudes scrutinized. However, the individual will benefit from the strong sense of community one finds in the HCC. Members share a feeling of involvement and unity in a collective enterprise. As a result, the church has an unusually high degree of identity.

The type of discipling method used by the HCC produces a leadership that is primarily self-generated. Most of the young men who are now shepherds in the HCC were formally members of the original flock pastored by Curlee. Members who aspire to become pastors have to be approved by the HCC leadership. Once, the approval is obtained and the discipling period is completed, these individuals are encouraged to disciple others. It is generally believed that their ability to find or draw others to their ministry is evidence of God's blessing.

Young pastors continue to be counseled and supervised by their shepherds. Thus, leaders maintain a servant relationship to their own pastors just as their flock is in a servant relationship to them. From an organizational standpoint, this arrangement acts as a system of checks and balances which helps to mitigate the chances of abuse or misuse of authority. In effect, every pastor or shepherd must answer to someone else. The system is not flawless, by any means. There have been some complaints of heavy-handed actions by shepherds from ex-members,[8] but the operation of authority is not left to the arbitrary dictates of any one individual.

The HCC readily admits that they are not for everyone. Potential converts must be willing to make considerable sacrifices to be a part of the church. They must be willing to enter into a covenant with a pastor and his flock. Many people are not willing or able to make these kinds of commitments. For these individuals, they say, there are thousands of traditional churches which will accommodate them. However, they claim, there is a significant number of people in the cities who desperately want and need a highly disciplined, religious life-style and community.

Case Study Two: Church of the Open Door, San Francisco

History and Development

Church of the Open Door, San Francisco, began as a mission project of another church, Church of the Open Door, San Raphael, in 1978. The San Raphael church was part of an association of five Open Door churches organized during the late sixties and early seventies. Their congregations originally were primarily countercultural youth who were converted during the Jesus movement in California. In fact, one of the senior pastors in San Raphael had worked with Arthur Blessit, a well-known leader in the Jesus movement.[9]

The need for another church related to the association of Open Door churches had arisen in San Francisco because of the defection of a previous group to the Shepherding movement. In the late seventies, the Jesus movement was winding down, and many people were looking for new emphases and directions in ministry. One such person was the former pastor of the Open Door Church in San Francisco. He disagreed with some policies of the Open Door churches and decided to leave, forming another house church ministry in south San Francisco. In the wake of the group's departure, it was felt that a vacuum had been created.

In January of 1978, a small group of people from Church of the Open Door, San Raphael, were sent to San Francisco to begin a new work. Three men were given the duty of sharing pastoral leadership. They rented a house and began operating home Bible studies at night during the week. On Saturdays, they went out into the streets in an effort to witness and recruit new members. Within a few months, they were prepared to begin holding meetings on Sundays. On Easter morning, with a nucleus of eleven people, they inaugurated a house church.

In the period which followed, the church was plagued by several setbacks and struggled to survive. One of the church's pastors was accused of stealing funds and forced to resign. The impact of the incident was disheartening to the group, and they experienced considerable turmoil as a result. The San Francisco church was also prohibited by the San Raphael church from initiating their own projects because of the group's disarray and lack of morale.

The deposed pastor was replaced by Bob Gaulden, who along with his wife, Carol, had been involved in another Church of the Open Door ministry in Redding, California. Over a period of two years, the church began to stabilize under the emerging leadership of Bob and Carol Gaulden. The church had experienced slow but steady growth and reached a core membership of about fifty-five.

In 1980, they received a letter from a church leader in Los Angeles. The letter described how the L.A. church had experienced dramatic growth through the application of church growth principles advocated by the faculty of Fuller Theological Seminary. The Los Angeles church membership had jumped from a few hundred to nearly seven hundred in only two years. In an effort to learn more, Robert Burns, one of the pastors of the San Francisco church, was sent to Los Angeles for a week. He observed the church, discussed the principles of their success with the leadership, obtained a printed manual for house churches, and returned to San Francisco ready to implement some of these ideas.

The San Francisco church found two strategies to be particularly successful. The first was a concentrated evangelistic effort in the streets and from door to door. The second was the deliberate creation of ethnic churches. In five months the church nearly doubled in size, from fifty-five to over one-hundred members. Between 1980 and 1984 the church continued to increase, although at a slightly less rapid pace. Still, the growth which did occur introduced a number of organizational problems.

Organization

Church of the Open Door, San Francisco, had about three-hundred members in 1984 and divided itself into three separate congregations, each with its own pastor. The largest group was made up of both Anglos and Chinese. This group had approximately one-hundred-and-sixty members and was pastored by Bob Gaulden. Robert Burns pastored the Filipino church which had approximately one-hundred members. Burns's wife is Filipino, which gave him a special identification with this ethnic group.

The third congregation was Hispanic, made up of mostly Central Americans, and was led by the church's other pastor, Eric Sorenson. These three congregations were further subdivided into small home group meetings during the week.

Unlike the HCC, Church of the Open Door has not employed different house church leaders for each small group. The
church's three pastors basically assumed leadership in all of the
small groups within their congregations. This facet of the organization was not by design, however. The supply of leadership,
they complained, was too limited. They were in the process of
training leaders to take over the small groups, but the immediate problem was that most of the membership was young,
predominantly high-school and college-age youth.

The house groups met on different nights of the week, and
the pastors met independently with each of them. This particular arrangement was very demanding upon the leadership's
time. However, they had hoped to eliminate this problem by
discipling members in the small home meetings. In the case of
the largest congregation, Carol Gaulden often met with some
of these groups to alleviate her husband's responsibilities. On
Sundays, each of the three congregations met separately. Two
of the congregations, the Filipino and the Hispanic, shared a
rented facility in San Francisco's Mission District and stag-
gered their Sunday worship services. The Chinese-Anglo congregation rented its own facility closer to downtown.
Periodically, all the groups met together for a corporate worship service or a joint ministry activity.

An additional feature of the largest congregation was that the
Chinese and Anglo members met separately during the week.
This did not appear to inhibit the harmony or unity of the
group. Indeed, it was our observation that ethnic barriers to
group unity were virtually nonexistent. Most of these young
Chinese-Americans were second-, third-, and fourth-generation
offspring of native Asians. They were fully westernized and
displayed the typical characteristics of language and dress one
might expect of California youth. Ethnic identity may have

been important in some respects, but it was apparent from the interaction between Asians and Anglos that these individuals had adapted to the pluralistic culture of the Bay Area.

Church of the Open Door has never owned any property. The reluctance to purchase property has been based on two considerations. One was practical. The membership came from ethnic neighborhoods in very diverse parts of the city. Thus, it has been difficult to find a central location that is convenient to all. In addition, many of the Spanish and Filipino members did not have adequate means of transportation. A second consideration involves the responsible use of available funds. With limited resources, the church did not want to be tied to a building debt. Bob Gaulden, the church's senior pastor, commented on this aspect of the problem.

> Well, if we had lots of money we could maybe buy some facilities for each of the churches to meet in. But we don't have that kind of money. If we bought one, it would be like we'd be putting all our resources into it. At this point, it would be misuse.[10]

A related reason for limited resources was due to the age factor of the congregation. As mentioned earlier, members were almost exclusively single, high-school, and college-age youth who had yet to begin occupational pursuits. Consequently, these youth could provide only minimum financial support. According to Burns, there were only ten married couples in the entire congregation at the time. However, the church had discovered something very important within the limitations of relative poverty: home group meetings provided an invaluable base for building relationships and developing a sense of ministry within the body of Christ. As one young woman remarked:

> I really like it because it's personal, and you get to know people,

and, you know, you can pray for one another, and it's more—it's not like this big meeting where you get lost or something.[11]

Pastor Burns discovered an equally important function of house groups. He found that home meetings had given him greater entree to certain ethnic groups such as Catholic Filipinos. Filipino youth may be prohibited by their parents from regularly attending a Protestant church. These youth may also be less comfortable in a large meeting. The house group poses neither of these obstacles. The home meetings typically were not found to be objectionable to parents, and Filipino youth found that they were not intimidated in small-group settings. Thus, one was given the distinct impression that they intended to preserve the home meetings. Indeed, Pastor Burns referred to them as "ideal."

> The ideal [is] home meetings. I love 'em. For instance, like the Monday night class, that's at my home, and it's real easy, especially working with the Filipinos because they are all Catholic. . . . On Sunday morning they visit, you know, and I come up to them afterward and I say, "Hey, tommorrow night, some people are going to be meeting at my house, and we are going to sit around and have some tea and talk and discuss the Bible, in my living room there, and I would like you to come too. Can you do it?" You know, like that. So usually you can get a yes, you see, because it's in the home, it's not threatening. It's relaxed, and then you can really minister, really change some lives because they don't have their guard up.[12]

Like the HCC, Church of the Open Door has found that home meetings may be used an an evangelistic tool. The prospect of conversion touches upon a sensitive issue of proselytizing among Catholics. Burns says no pressure has been put upon Filipinos to join the church. He appeared to be more concerned with personal conversions. Burns has a Catholic background himself and is ostensibly well prepared to deal with disapproving parents and families. Many Filipinos do join, of course, but parental approval has been sought by the church before this occurs.

The format of the house group meeting has been well ordered, even methodical. The night we attended the Chinese house meeting, Carol Gaulden was presiding. It met in an apartment of a Chinese family, all of whom participated. There were between thirty and forty people in the room. It was a larger crowd than had been anticipated. Carol called the meeting to order and welcomed all the visitors. After a few brief statements, the group began to sing and worship. Many of these youth appeared to be new converts and lent a considerable air of enthusiasm to the worship. Members clapped, sang, and raised their hands. The room was full of vocalized praise and shouts of "Thank you, Jesus," and, "Praise the Lord."

The scenario was strongly reminiscent of the Jesus movement, a phenomenon now more than a decade removed. Needless to say, it was not an abode for the timid; the feeling of excitement was contagious. This period of singing and worship lasted for about twenty minutes. At the end of this time, Carol asked for testimonies from persons who felt that God had performed some deed in their lives during the previous week. Several persons gave accounts of answered prayers, and the group was further invigorated and encouraged.

Following testimonies. Carol read several passages from the Bible and taught the group for a period of about a half hour. Group participation was also invited, and occasional insights were offered by members to support particular points or claims. Carol concluded her lesson and asked persons to divide into groups of three for private prayer. People shared prayer requests, and these were addressed in the small groups for a period of about fifteen minutes. Finally, the group sang another song and closed by holding hands in a collective prayer. After the meeting, most of the people in the room remained for informal fellowship. When we left a half hour later, many of these people were still there.

It should be pointed out that the church's heavy reliance upon house groups has not been without problems. While the groups have been effective for achieving both *koinonia* and growth, Church of the Open Door's greatest organizational problem has been too much decentralization. According to Burns, there had always been a problem of communication among the three congregations and their house groups.

> One of the problems we have had is communication. We can't communicate. Like, if there is a change in what's going on, it takes a couple of weeks for everybody to find out, *because there are so many different meetings.* Something may be announced properly in one meeting, may not be announced at all in another, or might be announced wrong in another. So one of the things we're going to do—since it's a unique problem because we have three churches, you see—is centralize the communication there.[13]

As Church of the Open Door developed and grew, it became very clear that it was necessary to make some organizational changes to accommodate the needs of the body.

Authority Structure and Beliefs

Like the HCC, Church of the Open Door stresses discipleship and the servanthood role of members but perhaps to a lesser degree. One does not find the intense focus on covenant relationships and all the implications discussed in case study one. These differences, however, can be exaggerated if not examined carefully. The groups share many similarities, including a principal dependence upon house groups with regard to an organizational structure, little or no property ownership, independence from denominational affiliations, and rather high expectations of commitment among members.

From the beginning, the three pastors of the Open Door Church had authority to make all decisions. Bob Gaulden was the senior pastor and the oldest of the three and thus took ultimate responsibility for the church. Members may have been asked to vote on key policy changes or major shifts in the direction of the church, but the pastors had the final authority. Members appeared to be satisfied with this arrangement. The age differential and the greater depth and experience of the pastors combined to agument their credibility as strong leaders.

As indicated before, there was a wide gap between the youthful inexperience of the laity and the seasoned, mature leadership of the pastors. It was the presence of this gap that represented one of the most critical problems facing the church: the need to develop new leadership. Most of the members were too young, both physically and spiritually, to assume all the responsibilities and duties of a leader. Burns indicated that this had been a factor inhibiting their growth.

> The main problem that we have encountered at any stage has been personnel. That has been the main problem, and that has been our prayer—to get the right personnel. The problem with starting a lot of little groups is: the quality degenerates if you don't have the proper personnel.[14]

Developing leadership internally takes time. Because Church of the Open Door is a house church and has had no denominational ties, there has been no institutional assistance, nor has there been any significant transfer growth of individuals with previous training or skills. The process of training leaders, Burns observed, was simply slower and more deliberate.

> A lot of churches are able to get personnel from other churches. They are able to get transfer growth. . . . People come into the city, and they like the church and they stay. For some reason, we have not been able to get that kind of growth. So all of the leadership we have comes through our own ranks—somebody we win to the Lord, and then they fill a spot. So that takes quite a bit longer.[15]

The process of developing responsible leadership cannot be rushed. Placing immature persons in roles of authority can be detrimental to the church body. Some adverse consequences already had been experienced by the church in this regard. "We learned the hard way," said Carol Gaulden, "that if you put people who are too young in leadership, they are like little Caesars." The church found that some persons would unintentionally abuse their positions of leadership, becoming too authoritative and demanding. Bob Gaulden stated that a member must be involved in the church for a minimum of two years before the individual could be eligible for leadership training. Church of the Open Door faced a critical challenge to be patient and permit the gradual development of stable and reliable leaders within its domain.

The church has been at a disadvantage because it has been loosely structured and barely organized. To its credit, however, the church has always been highly disciplined. It has had strict requirements for membership which helped the church to weather some of these crises.

Would-be members must complete a ten-lesson series on the church's doctrine, philosophy, organization, and goals before they can be considered candidates. The series, called the Foundation Program, lasts between twelve and fifteen weeks and is taught by one of the pastors. In addition, potential members must also share in the church's commitment and vision. They have to be willing to make extensive personal sacrifices and become involved in ministry activities on a regular basis. One's dedication and involvement must be demonstrated over a trial period of nine months in which the pastors determine the intentions and sincerity of each individual. According to Burns, the commitment levels of members must approach those of the pastors themselves.

> Now, as far as involvement in the program, we expect the member to have the same amount of commitment as the pastor of the church. After all, it is not the pastor's church, it is God's church. I don't have . . . loyalty to the church because it is my church, or anything like that. It's because it is God's work, and to love God and to serve the Lord is to love what He's doing and get involved in His program. . . . [W]e expect the same commitment from members as pastors. Though they may not have the same experience, or they may not have the same gifts, they may have different gifts, [but] as far as commitment and loyalty are concerned, it should be there, and that's shown by the ninth month. . . . The program of the church, at minimum, consists of Sunday morning attendance, prayer festivals, soul-winning programs, and laying down their lives in some other specific ways for other people in the church, like giving rides to meetings, being a volunteer, somebody who really wants to get into filling some need, filling some gap.[16]

After the trial period, a pastor will recommend an individual for membership to the body. Members then may vote on whether or not to accept the person in question. A majority vote determines acceptance. As yet, no one has ever been rejected. It is implied that anyone who has persevered to this point is usually quite sincere about his or her commitment. People who have not been serious or who have been unwilling to meet the demands of the church typically drop out before they ever reach a vote by the membership.

The reasons for such stringent requirements have been related to their goal of making disciples rather than simply attracting church members. Church of the Open Door has believed it will need a deeply committed group of individuals to stabilize the church and ensure its growth in the future. It has sought to make a significant impact upon the city of San Francisco. But it has no illusions about the difficulty of that task. They teach that Christianity is hard work, and that a price has to be paid. Members are told they may be ridiculed by their friends because they take their religion too seriously. They are asked to reorder their priorities and to seek the kindgdom of God first.

For instance, their Saturdays may be spent in activities such as street evangelism or prayer while their school friends enjoy leisure-time watching television, going to the beach, or just listening to music. One is impressed by the way in which Open Door members have had a no-nonsense attitude about their faith. There is little risk that members can be accused of what Bonhoeffer has called "cheap grace."[17]

New Developments

Since the original research was conducted on this church, which is reflected above, there has been a major change in the leadership and format of the group. Bob Gaulden and his Anglo-Chinese group have merged with the Novato Open Door Christian Church but remain as a San Francisco-based congregation completely separate from its original group. The Spanish-speaking group has merged with another Hispanic church in the city and has no further ties with Open Door. This left only the Filipino group with Robert Burns and Eric Sorenson as the copastors.

The division was primarily over the problem of leadership (evidenced in the foregoing discussion) and a difference in philosophy. Burns and Sorenson wanted to retain the original philosophy and style, and Gaulden wanted to go to a more traditional approach.

The present San Francisco Church of the Open Door is now largely Filipino. It has continued to grow impressively and presently has six weekly home group meetings which are called prayer festivals. In addition, the church has other house group meetings as a part of its larger church life. It now has more house groups than the original church which involved the large Anglo-Chinese group.

Even though the church is largely Filipino, it is not exclusively ethnic. Its language is English, and it is now reaching out to the larger community around it in the city. It is presently making an effort in the direction of Chinatown and the Tenderloin area, a principal residence of refugees from Southeast Asia: Vietnamese, Cambodians, and others.

The church continues its traditional emphasis upon membership and leadership training with the same high standards of commitment and involvement. Though the congregation meets weekly on Sunday in a rented facility, the home meetings are still the cutting edge of the church's life as it continues to grow despite radical changes in leadership and structure.

Because of its strong Filipino connection, it now has three small congregations in the Philippines with a total of some one-hundred members. The San Francisco Church has doubled its Filipino congregation, so that today it alone is as strong as the larger group was when the division came. This illustrates

the dynamics of these house groups and their ability to continue
to grow despite change and problems.

Notes

1. These ideas have appeared regularly in *New Wine* magazine at least since 1973. See also Juan Carlos Ortiz, *Disciple* (Carol Stream, Ill.: Creation House).

2. From an interview with Keith Curlee.

3. Ibid.

4. See Bill Ligon with Robert Paul Lamb, *Discipleship: The Jesus View* (Plainfield, N.J.: Logos International, 1979); Bob Buess, *The Pendulum Swings* (Indianola, Ia.: Inspirational Marketing, 1974).

5. See Tim LaHaye, *Battle for the Mind* (Old Tappan, N.J.: Revell, 1980); George Sweeting, *A National Call to Renewal* (Chicago: Moody, 1976); Rus Walton, *One Nation Under God* (Old Tappan, N.J.: Revell, 1975).

6. Interview with Keith Curlee.

7. Ibid.

8. Only a few of these accounts could be confirmed. They usually involved a claim that a shepherd overstepped his bounds in making some kind of unreasonable demand on an individual. See also Ligon, *Discipleship*.

9. Arthur Blessitt, Duane Pederson, and Jack Sparks are often considered to be the most influential figures during the early period of the Jesus movement. For example, see Ronald Enroth, Edward E. Ericson, and C. Breckenridge Peters, *The Jesus People: Old Time Religion in the Age of Aquarias* (Grand Rapids: Eerdmans, 1972); James T. Richardson, Mary W. Stewart, and Robert B. Simmonds, *Organized Miracles* (New Brunswick, N.J.: Transaction, 1979).

10. Interview with Bob Gaulden.

11. Interview with Robert Burns and several group members.

12. Ibid.

13. Ibid.

14. Ibid.

15. Ibid.

16. Ibid.

17. Dietrich Bonhoeffer, *The Cost of Discipleship* (New York: MacMillan, 1949).

7

The Nature of Religious Social Movements

The proliferation of house groups in their various forms has been so rapid in recent years that their spread can be considered a religious social movement. Recognition of this growth, however, has been obscured largely because the movement's structure is so decentralized, diverse, and segmentary.

A movement is typically viewed as something which has a clearly defined leadership and which is centrally directed and organized. It may not have all the bureaucratic administrative machinery that some formal organizations have, but most people believe that a movement still must possess centralized coordination and leadership. Very often, such direction is attributed to a single charismatic figure or a small elite group of leaders. When such structure and leadership are not apparent, it is mistakenly assumed that no real movement can exist. Indeed, what many people see in the growing number of house groups is only a randomly distributed outbreak of novel groups, quite unrelated to each other.

In this chapter, we want to show how the various sectors and groups are linked together as a movement and how the composition of their individual parts make up the movement as a whole. In doing so, we also show how the movement is growing and why its growth has received so little attention. In effect, we want to look at the dynamics of the house group movement at the *macro level.* In using this approach, we borrow theoretical and analytical concepts from social science, particularly the study of religious social movements, in an effort to gain further insight into the structure and growth of house groups.

Our social movement analysis relies heavily on the work of Luther Gerlach and Virginia Hine.[1] It is not simply coincidence that their study of the Neo-Pentecostal movement has special relevance for the house group movement. Much of the Neo-Pentecostal or Charismatic movement has taken place through small groups meeting in homes. Gerlach and Hine make this observation themselves.[2] The two movements are not identical, but there has been considerable overlapping which makes the study by Gerlach and Hine most helpful.

Having already discussed the diversity of house groups in a typology in chapter four, we now want to concentrate on three particular features of the movement: decentralization, segmentation, and networking. Following this, we will attempt to analyze the movement in its broader social and cultural context.

Three Features of Movement Organization

Decentralization

Decentralization in terms of authority refers to the dispersion of decision making. More people share responsibility. Conversely, centralization refers to the concentration of authority or decision making in the hands of a central group or unit. The house group movement is decentralized. Decision making in house churches and cell group networks is typically made at the level of the local church or community. The agglomeration of local groups is not tied together in regional, national, or international organizations linked by centralized polities. Even though some sectors such as the Shepherding movement seem to have a degree of centralization, they represent only a small part of the total movement. Some churches which have grown extensively also have designated regions of a city overseen by delegated personnel, but they still remain within the auspices of a local church. Linkages beyond the local church are typically cooperative rather than hierarchical.

Intra-movement ties are based primarily on a shared philosophy of organization and ministry, not a chain of command. Ideas, models, concepts, and techniques are perpetually being shared and exchanged among the autonomous movement components. Seminars, conferences, and training events are one of the means by which information and experiences are transmitted. Many groups or churches have a general understanding of how cell groups operate, but pastors continually invite new ideas for revision and refinement. They often seek specific details about how the groups can be improved.

Cho, for example, sponsors regular training events on the theoretical and operational aspects of home cell groups which are attended by religious leaders around the world. Such training seminars have become increasingly popular because they serve several functions. They not only assist in (1) educating and inspiring existing house groups, they also (2) create interest, (3) answer questions of churches considering home cell ministries, and (4) provide channels of movement assimilation and mutual identity.

One formal characteristic of decentralization is the absence of a solitary leader. There is no single leader of the house church movement. Neither is there a group of elite leaders who control the movement. There are widely recognized figures such as Cho, Larry Richards, Arthur Foster, Tommy Reid, Howard Snyder, and John Hurston who have had an important impact upon the movement. However, no one individual could be called the leader, and none of them could speak for the movement as a whole. Cho's influence has been extensive, and some even feel he is the father of the modern house group movement. But it is important to note that the cell group concept preceded Cho, even in recent years, as do Christian house group movements in general. Robert Raines advocated reshaping the church by adopting new structures such as *koinonia* groups (that is, cell groups) back in 1961, about four years before Cho reports being shown the idea by the Holy Spirit.[3] Moreover, in another book, Raines made reference to a "house church movement in Leeds, England" during the 1950s.[4] Joyce Thurman made a similar notation in her study of the house church movement in England.[5] Thus, we may safely assume that the present movement does not originate with Cho's ministry nor is it limited to his influence.

Obviously, there is no one individual who can make decisions that are binding upon all participants. This assertion may seem innocuous, but there are always some who believe that a movement must have a "true" leader. It is more accurate to say, however, that there are certain individuals who may exercise more influence than others. These persons may even articulate some basic tenents to which most participants subscribe. But they can only have authority in the sectors of the movement in which they are the organizational or ideological leader(s).

The decentralized nature of the movement strongly favors decision making at the local or grass-roots level. It is quite likely that the popularity of the house church movement is partially attributable to decentralization. John Naisbitt, in his book *Megatrends,* suggested that one of the major forces emerging in contemporary society is the widespread preference for decentralization in most social and political institutions.[6] Decentralization is preferable because it is more democratic and allows for greater participation by individuals. It may be suggested that the house church movement mirrors a shift toward decentralization in the larger society.

Decentralization is firmly evidenced by the movement's prevailing emphasis on delegation and diffusion of leadership. The house church movement is a *lay* movement, in every sense of the word. Participants generally adhere to the notion of the priesthood of believers. Laity are impelled to assume active roles in the small groups. They are urged to find and employ their spiritual gifts for the purpose of ministering to the needs of others. Each believer becomes a minister or laborer, and no one is made to feel spiritually inadequate or inferior because he or she lacks credentials or professional training.

This is in contrast to the passive observer who expects a professional class of clergy to perform all the work of the ministry. Laypersons are asked to take initiative, to be teachers and evangelists. The biblical metaphor of the body, which is so often stressed among house church groups, suggests that each person has an important function in the organism as a whole. Believers are said to have a measure of authority within themselves as given by Christ. It is critical to the idea of cell growth that individual members take some initiative to recruit new persons and to keep the group strong.

When groups grow and divide, new leaders are needed. Thus, there must exist some avenues by which able individuals may be cultivated for leadership and be given duties and responsibilities. A plurality of leadership is inherent in the home cell and house church models. Leadership roles are necessarily multiplied throughout the body. The art of pastoring is fostered, and the small ratios of pastor to group make indispensable a larger supply of leaders. The house group structure demands an increase in the number of leaders. Furthermore, the apportionment or distribution of pastoral functions among the laity is necessarily a process of decentralization.

Cho understands the significance of lay leadership. He devotes an entire chapter of his book to encouraging and motivating laity. The cell system is contingent upon effective lay pastors, and the host church, he says, must be able to provide firm support for these individuals. Recognition of their import is underscored by special events and ceremonies designed to honor cell group pastors at the Seoul church. These are augmented by routine leadership meetings which are guided by three criteria: (1) recognition, (2) praise, and (3) love.[7]

The house church movement, then, is dependent upon an ever-expanding reserve of leaders. Even at the highest levels, there is a plurality of leadership among various figures who have influence in whole sectors of the movement. Gerlach and Hine refer to such leadership as "polycephalous" or many headed.[8] Power, influence, and authority originate from many different sources, and it is hard to imagine that they could all agree on the particulars of a consensual organizational structure or form a central decision-making polity.

Theological and philosophical unity has been forged, to a degree, in a mutual effort to develop effective urban church models of ministry. From this has come a sense of shared identity and purpose. Foundationally, the movement components maintain solidarity through cooperation while utilizing individual initiative and leadership.

Segmentation

A segmentary movement organization is one in which various localized groups or cells are basically independent but can coalesce to form larger configurations or divide to form smaller units. Gerlach and Hine call these processes *fusion* and *fission.*[9]

All social systems are comprised of individual components, but in a bureaucratic, centralized system the components are always subservient to a center and function according to a prescribed chain of command. More importantly, new units or cells cannot be organized without the approval of a central administration. At the local or micro level, house churches and home cell groups have some centralization and supervision. But at the macro level, no such overarching organization exists. The various segments of the movement are separated by geography, social class, ethnicity, and religious backgrounds. Growth often follows cultural and geographical boundaries, as groups divide and multiply (fission), forming a vast network of distinct but interrelated cells.

One of the major factors contributing to segmentation is preexisting personal and social divisions. Movements often transform individuals and societies. They can dismantle old allegiances and create new ones. But it does not follow that all social relationships and cultural background factors can be eradicated. It is well known among students of social movements that recruitment frequently follows the lines of preexisting social relationships, such as friends or relatives.

As growth weaves along these previously established lines of association, they typically reflect the regionalism and ethnicity of the people involved. For example, house groups in Boston or Chicago will not have the same cultural milieu or regional flavor as those in the Deep South, say in Atlanta or Nashville. Hispanics in Los Angeles will not reflect the same ethnic tastes or interests as while Anglos in the midwestern cities of Tulsa or Kansas City, or as Blacks in Philadelphia. Ethnic and regional differences help create a segmented movement.

The same is true of socioeconomic and educational differences. Preexisting cleavages along the lines of occupation, income, and social status may act as channels by which the movement spreads. The movement may span all social class levels, but because social relationships or friendship networks tend to be more or less homogeneous in this regard, they can act as tributaries of the movement by which growth is accomplished. For example, one sociological observer contended that house churches have been more effective "among segments of the upper middle status."[10] This may well reflect segmental growth among upper-middle-class friendship networks in the Chicago area since the base-satellite churches in Texas, discussed in chapter four, were found to be effective among working-class persons.

The principle of growth along social class lines will hold true regardless of the income level. House groups can even spread among the very rich. This may be seen in a case we encountered in San Francisco. The pastor of a rather traditional Baptist church in Mill Valley, California, currently leads several house groups among the very affluent. The ministry began with only a few people meeting in the home of a wealthy couple in San Marin. As time elapsed, friends and neighbors were drawn to the house group and converted. The success of this group spawned others, and now it is only one of several that meet in the Bay Area. Many of these same individuals reportedly would not have graced the front steps of an institutional church. The inroads to this affluent community were made possible because of preexisting social relationships and lines of association.

Religious background or church affiliation also engenders segmentation. Established churches adopting cell groups will typically see growth occur along denominational boundaries. The strength of denominational allegiances vary and may be stressed by some more than others. But again, the preexisting divisions act as channels of expansion. Religious divisions feed house group growth into separate veins of the total church population. Each segment or unit has its own regulatory functions and its own style. Lutheran-based cell groups will differ from those of Baptist or Assemblies of God churches.

For example, house groups associated with Methodist or Episcopal churches are more likely to recognize and incorporate liturgical modes of worship (Communion, Lent, and so forth) than the "lower" or less liturgical branches of Protestantism.[11] Concomitantly, house groups based in Southern Baptist churches would be more likely to emphasize evangelism, as indicated by our case study earlier. Home groups that are tied to denominational churches will, in most instances, reflect their respective doctrinal traditions and beliefs in some form or another.

Similar cleavages within the Neo-Pentecostal Movement have been identifed by Gerlach and Hine. They found that new converts to the movement tended to separated from classical Pentecostal groups along several lines.

> As the movement spreads across class or cultural boundaries, new "Spirit-filled" Christians characteristically seek established Pentecostal sect churches in their cities, intending to join them in their worship services and to talk about the experience of the Baptism. The established Pentecostals eagerly welcome such converts, of course, interpreting their presence as a sign that the movement is indeed growing. But both groups generally discover that a truly rewarding association is hindered by differences not only in educational and socio-economic background, but also in theological orientations. Repeatedly, we have seen newly Baptized Pentecostals tend to withdraw and form their own independent groups; or, if they are Episcopal or Catholic groups containing sympathetic or participating clergy, they simply

meet regularly in their own churches with members of other non-Pentecostal churches who have had the Pentecostal experience.[12]

Segmentation and proliferation of cells may also be a result of geographical mobility. Individuals who are members of a house church group in one city may move to another city and be unable to find a similar arrangement. These individuals, therefore, may encourage their new church to begin home cell groups, or they may initiate home meetings themselves. The spawning of new groups creates growth in previously unaffected segments, and geographical mobility permits cell division and growth to transcend local settings. The proliferation of house church groups in this manner leads us to consider another feature of the movement: networking.

Networking

Networking (or reticulation) refers to the arrangement or formation of a network, which may be described as weblike, with crossing and intercrossing lines.[13] The house church movement can be characterized in this manner, in which the vast array of cells, or clusters of cells, form a network of intersecting relations and contacts. A weblike or reticulate organization has no absolute center but, rather, operates through the latticelike complex of local groups and cells. There are four levels at which networking occurs: (1) personal ties between members; (2) personal ties between leaders; (3) seminars, conferences, and workshops; and (4) theological or philosophical/ideological linkages.

(1) Personal ties between members of different local groups help form extensive social networks. Individual members frequently have close friends or relatives who belong to other house groups. Members may cross back and forth, visiting or

participating in the activities of friends' or relatives' groups. Some persons may even belong to more than one home Bible study or home fellowship group. As stated previously, a defining characteristic of house group forms such as home Bible studies and home fellowships is that members do not have to belong to the host church. They may belong to other churches while attending these types of house groups during the week. Both networking and integration are advanced as individuals expand participation to extra local groups or cells.

Similarly, a residential move to another part of the city may entail changing churches and locating new house groups. Old ties and friendships will persist even though residential or geographical mobility will disperse the various participants throughout a city or region. These personal ties can also be utilized by pastoral staff to compare different cell group programs or put leaders in touch with one another.

Another type of linkage is when a cluster of cells separate from the host church to form a satellite or sister church. Once again, there are often deep personal relationships which precede the division and typically supercede organizational segmentation. Family or friendship bonds reinforce channels of communication and reticulation at the local level.

(2) Personal ties between leaders may also link groups together in close association. In some cases, such ties may connect hundreds of groups across the country in loose or informal networks. Leaders of successful house church or cell group ministries frequently communicate with each other and monitor each other's progress. They regularly exchange correspondence and materials. Some churches have made available a reserve of cassette tapes, books, pamphlets, and training manuals to accommodate the steady influx of requests for materials by other pastors and churches. Because the house church move-

ment is still in its formative stages, there is a paucity of information about effective techniques and models. The "leadership exchange system" is one of the few means by which some churches or groups have access to this information. It is simply a word-of-mouth process and is consistent with the decentralized, segmentary nature of the movement we have described thus far.

(3) Conferences, seminars, and workshops are a third source of linkage for the movement. For the most part, these remain local or regional, but some have been national or international in scope. The Methodist-based House Church conferences held at Chicago Theological Seminary are one example as are the annual conferences held at the Yoido Full Gospel Church in Seoul, Korea.[14]

Such events strengthen movement ties and pull together resources and strategies for organization and growth. Many local churches sponsor regular training events or workshops on cell groups for their own personnel. These are often attended by other interested persons in order to procure needed information and upgrade their own efforts. Sometimes, churches may even pool their resources and hold joint workshops, sharing successes and failures for the mutual benefit of the other. An increasing supply of experts on small groups have been emerging from the seminaries and theological schools. Many of these are called upon as consultants or are asked to speak at seminars.

The number of conferences addressing the need for house groups has grown dramatically. Frequently, these are a part of a larger agenda covering the general topic of church growth. Indeed, it appears that the strategy of small home groups has become a fundamental part of church growth principles. Recently, we had the opportunity to hear representatives from the Fuller Institute for Evangelism and Church Growth and the

Institute for American Church Growth, and the inclusion of house groups was an integral part of both presentations. Cho has made a videotape on home cell groups, and one will frequently find this tape shown at conferences all over the country. John Hurston, a former missionary to Korea who worked with Cho's church, has continued to support the home cell concept in Southern California and has been active in several conferences and seminars. Dennis Corrigan, pastoral coordinator of the home cell groups at Church on the Way, Van Nuys, California, is also a frequent speaker. Both Hurston and Corrigan spoke at the National Church Growth Symposium in Los Angeles in August, 1983.

(4) Theological or philosophical/ideological linkage is the fourth means by which networks are developed. Participants share a common philosophy or orientation to ministry. House church groups reflect changing needs in urban society. They are more personal, flexible, and informal than most other structures. They offer a refuge from an impersonal, bureaucratic society; they are not rigid, but instead are relaxed, comfortable, non-intimidating and responsive to the needs of individuals.

In principle, many feel house groups are a biblical form which must play an important role in how we do church in the future. In this conviction, one finds a simple but powerful basis for unity in the house group movement. Moreover, it is this kind of ideology that is best adapted to the organizational diversity that exists. Despite personal, structural, and doctrinal differences that divide the groups, the conceptual commonality of house groups and the emphasis on lay leadership seem to touch the heart of solutions to contemporary problems in church and society. United in core belief, the diverse parts form a coherent whole, a distinct movement within the church today.

The House Group Movement in
Social and Cultural Context

Every generation of youth is, to some extent, a product of its culture and reflects the problems and struggles that face society and its citizens. The postwar generation of youth raised during the fifties and sixties was the first to grow up in a truly urbanized culture, with its mass communications and marketing, fear of nuclear holocaust, space explorations, computer revolution, and so on. Not coincidentally, it is this same generation that forms the nucleus of the current house group movement in the United States. American society has become increasingly urbanized and the economic division of labor more complex and specialized. From a sociological perspective, we should expect to see a correlation between the response (and needs) of this new urban generation and the new forms they advocate. Is it really surprising that they should decry the eclipse of community? Daniel Yankelovich, in his most recent book *New Rules,* pointed to evidence that the concern for community has increased among young Americans while at the same time, many are said to be more open about their religious faith.

> Our surveys also show some . . . evidence of a growing concern with community and caring relationships (for example, over the past several years, the number of Americans engaged in activities to create closer bonds with neighbors, co-religionists, co-workers, or others who form a community has grown by almost 50 percent). . . . Young people speak more openly of their religious beliefs and their concern for the future. In my interviews, people express a longing for connectedness, commitment, and creative expression.[15]

Toward the conclusion of the book, Yankelovich wrote:

In 1973, the "Search for Community" social trend, whose status
my firm measures each year, stood at 32 percent, meaning that
roughly one third of Americans felt an intense need to compensate for the impersonal and threatening aspects of modern life
by seeking mutual identification with others based on close
ethnic ties or ties of shared interests, needs, backgrounds, age,
or values. By the beginning of the nineteen eighties the number
of Americans involved in the Search for Community has increased to 47 percent—to almost half the population—a large
and significant jump in a few short years.[16]

Widick Schroeder, professor or Religion and Society at Chicago
Theological Seminary, stated:

> The environmental forces producing urbanization, industrial-
> ization, and bureaucratization are very strong and very perva-
> sive in contemporary America. These forces are rooted in
> technical reason. . . . Technical reason fosters the separation of
> spheres of the social order, the segmentalization of social roles,
> and the evaluation of human beings on the basis of their compe-
> tencies to perform specified tasks. It encourages proliferation of
> *secondary* relationships and a multiplicity of social groups
> which are primarily instrumental and affective-neutral.
>
> Human beings cannot live exclusively in such secondary
> groups, for they have needs for intimacy, sharing, caring and
> wholistic and integrating relations. These needs are best met in
> primary groups, and it seems to me the House Church is explor-
> ing one means of fostering such groups.[17]

Unlike their predecessors, the postwar generation has grown
up in a highly mobile society. Many have never known the
stable communities of rural and small-town America. The
house churches and home cell groups we have seen emerge in
the last fifteen years are not a temporary expression of a passing
fad or a remnant of a bygone counterculture. They represent
emerging forms which are a direct response to the problems
inherent in a complex, mass society. If we are wise, we will not

ignore these signals. Society is changing, and the church must change as well or lose its relevancy. Church structures should be malleable and adaptable to the changing needs of the people they seek to reach.

The very features of the house group movement analyzed in this chapter resonate changes in American society. In fact, we want to suggest that the continued viability of the movement is assured precisely because it is rooted in fundamental and widespread shifts in the larger culture. We want to offer support for this thesis by correlating features of the house church movement with major sociocultural transformations identified by research specialists monitoring these changes.

Decentralization, as observed earlier, is both a characteristic of the house church movement and one of the major social transformations discussed and analyzed by Naisbitt in *Megatrends*. Indeed, one may go well beyond Naisbitt to find supportive evidence for increased decentralization. Over the past two decades in America, there has arisen a basic distrust and suspicion of large, centralized bureaucracies. In the wake of industrial pollution, the covert dumping of toxic wastes, Watergate, and the scandals of bribery and price gouging among energy-rich oil companies, Americans have come away with very little faith in such corporate structures. Witness, for example the parade of films depicting the abuses of large bureaucracies (*All the President's Men, Three Days of the Condor, The China Syndrome,* or *Silkwood*). It may even be argued that such sentiment helped elect Ronald Reagan as president because of his stand against growing federal bureaucracy and his support for states' rights.[13] Centralized bureaucratic organizations are seen as too impersonal, too unwieldy, and lacking in accountability. In other words, they have a tendency to run amok over individual rights and human needs.

Americans dislike the feeling of powerlessness and lack of control over their lives. Decentralized organizational structures are appealing because they help diminish these problems and fears. Decentralization distributes power and permits greater input at the local level. Individuals are less apprehensive about participation in organizations of this type because they have more control over policy decisions, and, consequently, how such decisions will impact their lives.

Naisbitt argued that decentralization is "America's natural condition, with centralization emerging only in our recent industrial past. . . . But more importantly, strong central leadership is anathema to democracy."[19] He further contended that decentralization is a direct result of failures by "top-down solutions." These failures have caused increased social and political activity among individuals at the grass-roots level. "Neighborhood groups," he said, "are becoming more powerful and demanding greater participation in decision making."[20] According to Alvin Toffler, "Decentralized groups reflect the breakdown of machine politics and the inability of big government to cope with the wide diversity of local conditions and people."[21] Concomitantly, the decentralization trend in business, says Toffler, is "evident everywhere."

What is occurring in the spheres of politics and business is also occurring in the religious sphere. The new emphasis on indigenous lay leadership and the diffusion of neighborhood house churches mirror the decentralizing trend in the wider culture. The increased popularity of small groups among religious people has not developed in a vacuum. There is a parallel increase in small local groups in other areas of life: support groups, encounter groups, student groups, community action groups, consumer groups, self-help groups, and so on. Research by Yankelovich suggested that Americans are forging a new "ethic of commitment," involving a desire for "closer and deeper personal relationships."[22]

The absence of a premier leader in the house group movement also reflects the recent changes in attitudes toward organization and leadership in the larger society. Decentralization precludes the concentration of authority into the hands of a few. According to Naisbitt, this follows the shift away from centralization.

> We have no great captains of industry anymore, no great leaders in the arts, in academia, in civil rights, or in politics. That is because we followers are not creating those kind of leaders anymore. . . . We are creating leaders along much narrower bands and much closer proximity.[23]

Segmentation, as a trend, is best described as a reflection of both growing structural diversity and cultural pluralism. As society becomes increasingly urbanized, it is accompanied by greater economic differentiation, cultural heterogeneity, and the political coexistence of competing interest groups.[24] In traditional societies or communities, social relations were characterized by similitude and conformity to a single, unified set of values and beliefs. But modern societies are characterized by greater individualism and the segmentation of life in all aspects.

Modern society invites high social and geographical mobility, an international economy, and occupational roles based on technical competence rather than kinship. Urban life features multiple religious, ethnic, and racial groups thus creating a plurality of values, beliefs, and life-styles. Though America has been described as the "great melting pot," research clearly demonstrates that "the ethnic, racial, and religious enclaves of the city have not . . . disappeared."[25]

In addition to the obvious divisions produced by social class, American pluralism also takes the form of regionalism. Without other strong sources of identification, people often attach themselves psychologically to regional areas of the country. A recent study by John Shelton Reed, professor of sociology at the University of North Carolina, showed that Southerners continue to have a distinct sense of sectional identity, even within the context of the "New South."[26] Survey research also shows that New Englanders and people on the West Coast are consistently more liberal with regard to social attitudes than other regions of the country.[27]

Naisbitt employed the term *new regionalism* to describe these powerful and pervasive sectional loyalties. He sees this development as a part of the decentralization process. The massive size and cultural diversity of the nation lends itself more favorably to regional and local sentiments.

Networking or reticulation is the third characteristic of the house church movement. This corresponds to the shift in society away from hierarchial organizational structures and is closely related to decentralization. It is noteworthy that Naisbitt turned to the work of Virginia Hine to locate "the best image of (reticulate) structures." He noted particularly Hine's description of networks in terms of "a badly knotted fishnet" in which the knots (or groups in our case) are of varying size and are all linked to one another.[28]

> What needs to be added is that networks are infinitely more complex because they are three-dimensional in nature.
>
> Networks emerge when people are trying to change society, said Hine. "No matter what the cause, the goals, or beliefs, and no matter what type of movement it is—political, social, religious . . . whenever people organize themselves to change some

aspect of society, a non-bureaucratic but very effective form of organizational structure seems to emerge."[29]

It should be said that much of Naisbitt's discussion of networking is speculative and even esoteric.[30] In any case, the most important point he made is that networks cut across traditional institutional boundaries and form a relational complex more readily open to social innovation and change. Indeed, they frequently are the vehicles of that change. Because networks are composed of localized cells or groups, they are more likely to be in touch with the changing attitudes and needs of the urban population than hierarchical structures. Most social or political movements begin this way. Networks form horizontal links between groups of relatively equal (little) power and similar beliefs and convictions. Independently, these groups have a small impact upon society. But taken together, they demand our attention and deserve a careful ear.

It is the cellular structure of social movements that often cause people to dismiss them as organizationally fragmented and thus ineffective or unimportant. But this belies the nature of modern social movements. Gerlach and Hine have shown that networks are well adpated to highly complex societies. They are especially adapted to spread the movement across class and cultural lines, penetrating all different levels and segments of society. Moreover, since the movement is thoroughly decentralized and segmented, the error of one leader, or the failure of one cell or segment, does not jeopardize the rest of the movement. Members of any one group can disband and reorganize under new leadership or be absorbed by other groups.[31] Reticulation can be a distinct advantage to a social or religious movement. According to Gerlach and Hine:

When the success of movements is reported as having oc-

curred "because of" rather than "in spite of" organizational
fission and lack of [structural] cohesion, we will have come to
understand the nature of movement dynamics much more clearly. Organizational unity is functional in a steady-state social
institution designed to maintain social stability and the status
quo. Segmentation . . . [is] functional in a social institution
designed for rapid growth and the implementation of social
change.[32]

The elements of change embodied in the house group movement are tied to the necessity of sociocultural adaptation. The
house group seeks to relate anew the basic principles of Christianity to a growing urban and unchurched world. It attempts
to change only the humanly constructed obstacles to outreach
and genuine community. Joyce Thurman contended that the
movement in England is anticlerical. She saw this as a major
thrust of the movement. However, it might be more accurate
to say that the movement protests hierarchial structures that
inhibit the gospel. For the most part, the house group movement protests the rigid inability of certain church forms to
relate to new generations of people in the cities. If religious
institutions lose sight of their purposes and seek only to perpetuate forms and traditions (old wineskins), they become use-
less. Ultimately, the movement affirms the vitality of
Christianity, showing that it is more than the structures or
traditions that have been identified with it. As the faith of new
generations transforms the channels of communication and the
expressions of commitment which house that faith, outsiders
will become persuaded by efforts to make the gospel pertinent
and meaningful to their own lives, in their own surroundings.

Notes

1. Luther P. Gerlach and Virginia Hine, *People, Power, Change: Movements of Social Transformation* (Indianapolis: Bobbs-Merrill, 1970).

2. Ibid., p. 3.

3. Raines, *New Life in the Church.*

4. Robert Raines, *Reshaping the Christian Life* (New York: Harper and Row, 1964), p. 10.

5. Joyce Thurman, *New Wineskins: A Study of the House Church Movement* (Bern: Verlang Am Main, 1982).

6. John Naisbitt, *Megatrends: Ten New Directions Transforming Our Lives* (New York: Warner, 1982), pp. 97-130.

7. Cho, *Successful Home Cell Groups,* pp. 135-144.

8. Gerlach and Hine, *People, Power, Change,* p. 35.

9. Ibid., p. 42.

10. W. Widick Schroeder, "A Sociological and Theological Critique of the House Church Movement," ed. Arthur L. Foster. *The House Church Evolving* (Chicago: Exploration Press, 1976), p. 54.

11. Bonnie Niswander, "Rebuilding a Congregation Through the House Church," ed. Arthur L. Foster, *The House Church Evolving* (Chicago: Exploration Press, 1982), pp. 81-97.

12. Gerlach and Hine, *People, Power, Change,* p. 44.

13. Ibid., p. 55. The authors use the term *reticulation* rather than networking in this source.

14. See Introduction in Foster, *The House Church Evolving.*

15. Daniel Yankelovich, *New Rules: Searching for Self-Fulfillment in a World Turned Upside Down* (New York: Bantam, 1981), p. 9-10.

16. Ibid., p. 248.

17. Schroeder, "A Sociological and Theological Critique of the House Church Movement," pp. 53-54.

18. Naisbitt, *Megatrends,* p. 102.

19. Ibid., p. 99.

20. Ibid., p. 113.

21. Alvin Toffler, *The Third Wave* (New York: Bantam, 1980), p. 258.

22. Ibid., p. 247.

23. Naisbitt, *Megatrends,* p. 101.

24. William M. Newman, *American Pluarlism: A Study of Minority Groups and Social Theory* (New York: Harper and Row, 1973).

25. Ibid., p. 77.

26. John Shelton Reed, *Southerners: The Social Psychology of Sectionalism* (Chapel Hill, N.C.: University of North Carolina Press, 1983).

27. *The Connecticut Mutual Life Report on American Values in the 80's: The Impact of Belief* (Hartford: Connecticut Mutual Life, 1981).

28. Naisbitt, *Megatrends,* p. 196.

29. Ibid.

30. Some of this chapter exceeds analysis based on empirical data and simply amounts to wishful projections. One problem is that Naisbitt assumes that individuals have more control over their lives than they really do. For a critical review of *Megatrends,* see Arthur G. Neal and Theodore H. Groats' review published in *Contemporary Sociology,* 1984, vol. 13, issue 1, pp. 120-22.

31. Gerlach and Hine, *People, Power, Change,* p. 77.

32. Ibid., p. 64.

8
Leadership and Authority in Christian House Groups

The character of any group is heavily influenced by the nature of its leadership. This is true for all social groups, but the critical role of leadership takes on added significance in an informal setting where bureaucratic rules, job descriptions, and corporate bylaws do not exist to channel decision making. In house groups the leader can only remain the leader if he or she is accepted by the members. Without this acceptance and trust, the group may dissolve. In this chapter we look at the role of leadership and authority with the purpose of probing the complex relationship between leader and follower.

Charismatic Authority

The leadership of any formative movement tends to be charismatic. We use the term *charisma* in its sociological connotation, of course, rather than to mean spiritual gifts in the biblical sense. Charismatic authority refers to a power relationship between leader and follower based on the *person* of the leader rather than on the legal office held or the longstanding tradition behind the role. Charismatic leaders lead by virtue of certain outstanding characteristics which have drawn followers to them.

Among house churches many charismatic leaders exist.

Some oversee many churches while others may pastor only one church. They have collected followers by virtue of their engaging personalities, perhaps an aura of spirituality, insightful teaching, and often through a genuine sense of personal warmth and caring. They lead and are followed because of these abilities, not because the position of pastor or some other title has been created for them. Who they are is much more important to their authority than what they are called.

Home cell groups may also be led by charismatic individuals, but this is not always true. Leaders of cell groups can be assigned in the same manner as Sunday School teachers by some churches, and in such situations what little authority is held by the leader rests in the position of cell group leader rather than in his or her person. We can also state, however, that the most effective home cell group leaders are those with a special gift for this type of ministry and who are able to win members to the group rather than rely on their assignment from the larger church. In fact, the effective home cell group approximates a small movement.

Who are the charismatic leaders of the house group movement? There are too many to mention, of course, and most are not household names. The movement has produced no great preachers or evangelists like Billy Graham or Luis Palau, but it has produced outstanding teachers and pastors with excellent organizational and administrative skills. When such skills are combined with dynamic personalities, the leaders who possess them become doubly effective and play a major role in the enormous expansion of home-related worship.

Paul Yongii Cho, pastor of the Yoido Full Gospel Church of Seoul, Korea, is a case in point. His vigorous style and spiritual demeanor magnifies his strong leadership qualities as a senior pastor, a church-growth theoretician, and an organizational genius. Although he is a local pastor, the unusual success of the home cell groups in his ministry has catapulted him into an international figure who is sought after as a speaker all over the world.

In a real sense, Cho has become a charismatic leader for the larger house group movement while remaining in an institutional setting. Even in his own church, Cho has become something more than a pastor. The fact that no other church in the world has begun to achieve the growth of the YFGC must be attributable, in part, to the unique charisma of Cho's leadership.

A national leader related to the shepherding movement who exhibits charismatic qualities is Bob Mumford. Mumford's image is basically that of a teacher, though he demonstrates masterful skills as a platform speaker. In person and on tape, his adroitness for identifying issues at the heart of personal crises of faith, as well as his self-flagellant humor, make Mumford an appealing and endearing personality. Many view Bob Mumford as a kind of "unofficial" spokesman for the shepherding movement.

At the local level, strong leadership qualities are also evident in Dennis Peacocke, a regional leader of the shepherding movement in the San Francisco Bay area of California. Peacocke exhibits a strong personality which combines able speaking gifts, penetrating acumen, a visionary spirit[1], and administrative skills as a leader. He has attracted leaders of preexisting house churches and incorporated them into a larger system of shepherding churches. In a sense, Peacocke is a charismatic leader to the charismatic leaders of the San Francisco Bay house churches.

Among Southern Baptists, Ralph Neighbour of Houston provides another form of leadership for the house group movement. He is a theoretician, a communicator, and a practitioner. His personal and literary influence has made an international impact on the movement, and he continues to play all three roles with great energy. Neighbour often operates as a consultant in helping churches implement home cell groups. Pastor Tony Rosenthal, whose home cell group strategies in the greater San Francisco Bay area are beginning to attract national recognition, is another charismatic leader at the local church level. Rosenthal has demonstrated extensive resourcefulness and energy in generating a network of home groups from a single Bible study in a few short years.

In the house church movement of Great Britain, some outstanding charismatic leadership types have emerged in various groups. Bryan and Keri Jones of the Harvestime Churches, B. W. North of the North Churches, and Sidney Purse of the Church at South Chard (Somerset) are some of the key personalities behind the movement.[1]

The Dilemma of the House Church

A charismatic leader can fuel a movement but cannot guarantee its stability and permanence. In the early stages of a movement, a leader wins converts who are attracted to his or her leadership and message. As the movement grows, the leader trains disciples, and they take on the major responsibility for recruitment. Eventually, it becomes less and less realistic for the group to depend totally on the original leader for every decision and directive. New members may have little contact with the leader and thus cannot feel the same charismatic attraction as did the early converts.

Other concerns include the leader's eventual death or retirement and the future direction of the group. The group eventually begins to yearn for stability, and a charismatic leader cannot provide it. Thus, one of the primary dilemmas of the house church is how to achieve stability and yet remain vital, retaining the characteristics which will continue to attract new converts. A second dilemma is how to sustain vitality without "going off the deep end" theologically.

The typical approach house churches take to the stability dilemma is to begin the process of "routinization of charisma." This means that the group tries to change the source of their leader's authority from the person of the leader to the office he or she holds. The step from a prophet to a pastor is a large one; but if the group is ever to achieve long-term stability, it must be taken. This is not to say that the charismatic nature of the leader's personality diminishes or that charismatic authority is ever fully replaced by a form of bureaucratic authority. Instead, the authority of position is added to the authority of the person —at least for the original leader. This helps to insure that whatever happens to the leader, the group will not die. A new leader will be selected to fill the position which was vacated.

The second dilemma is much more difficult. If people trust a leader completely and have forsaken all to follow this person, then they will continue that trust regardless of how bizarre his or her ideas become. "Power tends to corrupt," as the saying goes, "and absolute power corrupts absolutely."[2] The charismatic leader of a house church, especially one which is autonomous and is not connected to other organizations or a denomination that can help correct excesses, runs a greater risk of deviance. This is how cults emerge.

The Dilemma of Home Cell Groups

Home cell groups face a different set of problems in dealing with charismatic leadership. Their basic dilemma is in how to contain charismatic leadership within a basically conservative institution. A degree of charisma is an advantage for the leader of a cell group in that such qualities help attract newcomers and also help secure continued interest and commitment. This is not to say that charisma is essential in the home cell group. It clearly is not. At the same time, however, the charismatic cell group leader is apt to be more effective in his or her leadership role.

Charismatic leadership in the home cell group can also be a problem. For example, a problem of divisiveness may arise if the leader's commitment to the host church is not very strong. An independent-minded leader, influenced by the adulation of his or her followers, may come to the conclusion that the group does not need the host church and may attempt to break away, taking followers along.

In some instances a leader may also begin a process, which could be called "theological drift," in which the theology of the leader begins to diverge from acceptable guidelines of church doctrine and faith. A group of adoring followers may find strange new theological concepts exciting (rather than heretical) and follow their leader with a blind sense of trust. Admittedly, however, such cases are rare.

At another level, there may only be a tension between the cell groups and the larger church organization. Some church members may feel the cell groups are too independent or that their expressive nature may lead to excessive displays of emotion or behavior. Problems are especially likely if the senior pastor is not wholeheartedly committed to the cell groups. If they are assigned exclusively to a staff person who specializes in this ministry and subsequently ignored, the pastor loses touch with the groups. The problem can be avoided largely through adequate supervision and care. Unfortunately, when the groups are criticized by tradition-minded members as being "too loose" or "out of control," the pastor may overreact and kill the ministry.

Charismatic leadership in the home cell group can be both a solution to and a source of problems. The problems can be overcome, however, and the possibility of division or theological drift should not deter churches from pursuing this type of ministry. As we have seen, some churches have been quite successful in managing the tension between control and freedom.

General Leadership Characteristics

Styles of Leadership Organization

In all home cell group organizations and in most other house groups, the local group leader does not stand alone. Instead, there is a leadership hierarchy which presides over this local leader. One of the most sophisticated arrangements we have seen has four distinct levels. The Elmbrook Church of Milwaukee illustrates this scheme (see chapter 5). Under the senior pastor is a pastoral coordinator of the neighborhood groups. He supervises eight regional shepherds who train and oversee the fifty-nine leaders of the home cell groups.

This leadership is exercised at the following levels: (1) the level of general pastoral oversight; (2) the level of specific pastoral oversight and coordination; (3) the level of coordination and training; and (4) the final level of guiding the house group in the function for which it has been designed.

The Yoido Full Gospel Church has a similar chain of command in its various leadership levels. However, since cell groups number in the thousands in this church (fifty thousand at last count), it is a much more complicated operation. Although the same four levels exist (senior pastor, district leaders, subdistrict leaders, home cell leaders)—three fourths of the full-time pastoral staff are involved at the district and subdistrict level, with the pastor filling both senior pastor and cell group coordinator roles.[3]

In the house church, we see a leadership heirarchy in a much different form. From an organizational perspective, this hierarchy may not seem to exist. Yet in most cases the group and its leader are not entirely independent. Some house churches may be affiliated with a denomination. If so, they relate to the denominational hierarchy in much the same manner as a typical institutionalized church. Other house churches are federated and form a collectivity somewhat looser than the average denomination. Here the leader may only relate to other church leaders in the federation and lack any true supervision by a bishop or judicatory head. In many other instances, however, such federated house church leaders and independent house church leaders may be part of a well-defined shepherding network.

In the shepherding system, the hierarchy is not a formal one. Instead, the various leaders in the network submit voluntarily to one another in a hierarchical arrangement. The relationship is based on trust rather than on bureaucratic structure. This form of leadership organization may seem loose and unstable, but in operation it approximates a very structured bureaucratic system—yet without the accompanying flaws of bureaucracy. It may lack permanence at this point, but we expect that before the trust and commitment fade, it will resemble a more conventional bureaucratic hierarchy.

Leadership Development

One of the most amazing aspects of the home cell group movement has been the phenomenal rate at which leadership has developed. The astounding rate of the proliferation of cell groups at the Yoido Full Gospel Church staggers the imagination—especially when we consider that new groups can only emerge as new leaders are trained. How has it been possible to develop fifty-thousand cell group leaders in the twenty years since the groups were first formed? There are various explanations.

One answer is that through the use of women in leadership positions, the church has not been restricted by a limited supply of willing or available men. Another factor is that leaders are trained to serve a specific group of known friends and companions rather than an abstract cluster of strangers. Since leadership emerges from the group, it presupposes a degree of familiarity and ease about the training process. Many assumptions about what constitutes leadership (especially as we have traditionally perceived it in the Western church) are not only challenged but are demonstrated to be irrelevant in the operation of this dynamic system of spiritual development and church growth. Perhaps the most significant factor is that small home-centered groups provide the intimate atmosphere (all other factors being equal) conducive to maximum leadership development (that is, at the level which is needed).

In home-related worship, almost every Christian is a candidate for leadership, although, obviously, all do not develop into group leaders. This, in part, explains why some home fellowship groups seem to be able to function even without a recognized leader. Leadership emerges at different times, at different levels, in different ways. No one is called the leader. The members complement one another. This is the major point Paul made when he spoke of the church as the body of Christ. The body constitutes the different parts whose proper and separate functions make possible the meaningful functioning of the whole (1 Cor. 12:14).

The Covenant Church of Houston and other groups of the so-called shepherding movement are not as dependent on an ever-increasing supply of leaders as are large churches organized around home cell groups. Nevertheless, the emergence and development of leadership at various levels is inherent in and integral to the operation of a house church movement. Once the first house groups are established in an area and are operative under their unique leadership structure, however simplified in its beginning, the leader encourages group participation. Part of the training the leader receives is in how to discern leadership potential in a group and how to set in motion the principles which will incite this potential and consequently develop it. In the most effective systems this dynamic transpires continuously as the groups meet and develop from week to week. The coupling dynamic of the trained head and heart of the leader and the high motivation stimulus of the spiritual group process help to explain the efficiency with which group leaders have emerged in house group movements.

Chapter 5 has outlined the eight phases of leadership development from a house group member to a regional shepherd found in the Elmbrook model. In this model, leadership potential is first identified, and then one is given special responsibilities in the group. He or she then will be asked to lead a group on special occasions. Subsequently, one will be invited to a session of a leadership training class. A personal interview will follow. If this is favorable, one then undergoes a thirteen-week training period. He or she then becomes a house church leader. His or her training continues; and if potential is discovered, one will then be groomed for a position as regional shepherd.

Efficiencies of Lay Leadership

The clergy-dominated Christianity of the Western world has widened the gap between clergy and laity in the body of Christ. This division of labor, authority, and prestige is common when a professional clergy exists and generally develops so slowly that it goes unnoticed. The pastor-shepherd has evolved gradually into the role of clergy-performer who is hired by the church as their "Sunday-before-dinner speaker," their witness to the community, and their sickbed comforter. Simultaneously, the priesthood of believers has evolved in the direction of an audience which consumes religious truth but does not act on it. The Christian faith is weakened by this violation of the *laos*, "people of God," which has thwarted the New Testament pattern of developing spiritual gifts in the whole body.

There has been little challenge or necessity to develop lay leadership in most mainline churches. Preaching, religious education, music, record keeping, visitation, counseling, and sacraments are mostly performed by or led by professionals. Laypersons are only needed to follow and to teach (and very little of that in churches which lack a strong tradition of Adult Sunday School). House churches and home cell groups reverse the direction of this trend towards professional leadership and put a primary emphasis on the lay leader.

The house church type will usually have an ordained pastor (if the group ordains its clergy); and even though clergy may serve as house group leaders in a variety of house church and home cell group models, the overwhelming majority of group leaders will be laypersons. When we consider the vast network of home cell groups sponsored by the Yoido Full Gospel Church and other churches which follow the same basic design of home meetings, we must conclude that to a significant degree it is a lay movement. Not only are laypersons the leaders of nearly all home cell groups, but often laypersons serve in a regional coordinating capacity in larger house group systems. Without this grass-roots lay involvement and without a significant network of lay leaders, the house group movement never would have emerged, and it certainly would not be the vital phenomenon it is today.

The Significant Place of Women

Even though some modern house group ministries do not use women at any level of leadership (except in ministry to women), some of the most dramatic and effective groups have found a significant place for women. This has been important because the proliferation of cell units creates a need for more leaders, and it becomes especially critical that a church not eliminate 50 percent of its potential small-group leaders on the basis of sex. It may not have enough male leaders to perpetuate the growth of the cell groups.

The Yoido Full Gospel Church has a significant place for women as home cell leaders. Pastor Cho, inspired by what he saw in the New Testament pattern in the prominent leadership roles of such women as Phoebe and Priscilla, shared his feelings with his congregation. Both women and men responded to the challenge. But as the cell concept flowered into reality, women, in time, became more prominent than men as home cell leaders —approximately two thirds of the cell leaders are women.[4] Cho observed that "churches which do not utilize the ministry of women are suffering greatly in thier overall growth and development."[5]

In other churches with home cell ministries, women play an important role as regional directors. They oversee the cell groups in a defined sector of the city, train new leaders, deal with problems which emerge, and help to create new units.

Through its placement of women in leadership roles, the house group movement in the United States has begun to overcome the tendency of white evangelical churches to underutilize women. Liberal mainline groups have recently channeled women into ministerial positions, and in black churches various administrative roles have long been the province of women. Yet conservative white churches and many sectarian groups have been unable to find significant leadership roles for women.

Affirmation of the Pastoral Role

The house group movement has helped to recover the biblical role of "the pastoral" in church leadership. Originally, the pastoral concept of spiritual leadership basically carried the idea of "caring"—drawing from the analogy of the shepherd caring for the total needs of his sheep: food, shelter, protection, and so forth. The concept was especially appropriate in biblical times because of the deep, personal "love-relationships" the shepherd developed with his flock. Also, in the Old Testament "shepherd" was used to designate the spiritual (caring) quality of leaders such as prophets, priests, and kings. Jesus, in His life role and in His teachings, brought this idea to a sublime level, especially in John 10. This was further accented in the New Testament through Jesus' injunction to Peter ("Feed my sheep," John 21:15-17) and Paul's admonition to the Ephesian elders ("Take heed . . . to all the flock, . . . to care for the church of God," Acts 20:28). The pastor (shepherd) was one of the leadership roles or functions in the New Testament (Eph. 4:11).

A major problem historically and contemporaneously is that the New Testament leadership roles and functions, which were often interchangeable, have been hardened into sacerdotal positions and offices of prestige and power. Essentially, we are left with cultural and historical factors which now determine the concept and function of pastor. The role has come to signify the idea and function of administrative head (in popular parlance, "the boss") rather than the leadership of caring, though we retain lip service to the notion.

Though a few of these aberrations have been carried over into some house group movements, by and large the movement has helped us to recover the biblical leadership role of caring which was originally meant by "pastoring" and "shepherding" (see Matt. 9:36; 1 Pet. 2:25; 5:2-3; Rev. 7:17).

Although the term *pastor* is usually reserved for the administrative head of the church, often with the designation "senior pastor," and for the coordinator (pastoral coordinator) and the regional coordinators—trainers (regional pastors)—the term in its biblical meaning may be more appropriately applied to the house group leaders. They are the real pastors, officially or unofficially. Cho has said it well, "The cell leader becomes a kind of pastor. . . . The cell leader knows each of the members of his group and can relate personally to their joys and problems with a kind of familiarity that a senior pastor cannot develop."[6]

The Depth of Commitment Inspired by the Leadership

The very nature of a small group requires a higher commitment level than that which tends to exist in larger, less defined, more impersonal churches. If one is uncomfortable with this closeness and the commitment it implies, he or she will soon leave. Thus, those who remain and constitute the group will reach a strong commitment level by the very nature of the small-group setting. When the spiritual dynamic augments the process, the potential for commitment becomes even greater, with the spiritual graces giving meaning and depth to the natural small-group process.

Cho and other leaders, certainly those of the shepherding movement, are very hesitant to credit the effectiveness of their house groups simply to the small-group process itself and to the operational efficiency of the house group systems which they have helped to develop. Cho emphasizes the prominence of prayer, ministering to needs, and studying and "living" the Word of God as some of the major elements that make this system work in his church.[7]

Submission vs. Supervision: Contrasting Paradigms of Authority

One of the key areas of controversy in the house group movement is in the particular type of authority system employed to direct an individual group toward its goals. This controversy has largely centered around the form of government used by the so-called shepherding movement. Not all house churches are part of this movement, of course, and not all exhibit a form of authority based on submission. At the same time, however, the house church movement in the United States has come to be identified with the shepherding concept and is often judged on this basis.

Before we can evaluate the shepherding system, it is necessary to contrast its authority system with its major alternative. The shepherding paradigm operates on the principle of submission while most other examples of house groups operate on the principle of supervision. Both types are strategy oriented. Both are preoccupied with discipleship. Both project a leadership chain of command through which its authority principle is able to operate efficiently and effectively. There is, therefore, a kind of hierarchical arrangement in both systems. However, despite the striking similarity of the overall design and the fundamental principles at work, the two systems are distinctly different in their orientation and philosophy.

Let us now examine the two different systems in terms of their contrasting orientations and philosophies. In the submission paradigm, the focus of authority is *in* the person of the leader; in the supervision paradigm, authority is channeled *through* the leader. Both systems acknowledge ultimate authority as being in God. However, in immediate and practical terms, the submission system locates the authority directly in the leader as part of a relational connection which goes finally to Christ. In the supervision system, however, persons see the leader as a symbol which represents the authority of the church and ultimately of Christ.

In terms of loyalty, persons who submit to other persons as authority figures are loyal primarily to their shepherd and secondarily to the group and the cause it espouses. By contrast, persons who are under supervision are loyal primarily to the cause which the group embodies and secondarily to the persons who lead in the advancement of that cause.

Community is achieved in one system by concurrent, pyramidal connections to the leader and in the other by a common purpose. The submission idea is consequently more directly relational and indirectly functional in its orientation, and the supervision idea is more directly functional and indirectly relational in its orientation.

From an organizational perspective, the submission principle is similar to monastic orders where one relates directly to a brother or sister superior. The supervision principle, however, fits more the corporation model where one relates to the purpose of the company (community).

In terms of its relational aspect, seen from a theological

perspective, the submission system is more paternal, and the supervision system is more fraternal in orientation. The former is more sacerdotal, with an emphasis on levels of spirituality; the latter emphasizes the priesthood of the believer, seeing its leaders as fellow priests in a common spirituality under Christ.

The submission idealogy subscribes to the master-servant relationship (see the interpretation of Keith Curlee of the Houston Covenant Church in chapter 6). The supervision ideology holds to a common servanthood under a divine Master and sees the New Testament principle of authority operative in servanthood, not mastership.

From a governmental viewpoint, the submission school is more oligarchic with rule being invested in a few. The supervision school is more democratic with rule being invested in the people (the group). Viewed from the perspective of classical church polity, the submission model is more episcopal, with authority located in the oversight of the clergy. The supervision model is more congregational, with authority located in the consensus of the believing community. From a practical perspective, each system at times usually has to operate from a presbyterial principle, with elders and/or deacons serving, if not as a governing body, as a leadership community guiding the community at large.

From a strategic point of view, the submission orientation is more developmental, seeing evangelism as inherent in the process of growing the body of faith. The supervision orientation is more directly evangelistic in its orientation with nurture seen as a means to and as a result of evangelism. Some supervision systems are not as directly evangelistic as others, though all of them see evangelism as central. The submission systems seem to let evangelism happen as it will.

The supervision model seems designed more to augment existing religious institutions, trying to make up for what is missing in the traditional churches. On the other hand, the submission model seems more consciously counterinstitutional, with a sense of bringing something new or recovering something which has been lost in traditional Christian churches and institutions. Although the submission groups cooperate with others in varying degrees and levels, they are basically nondenominational.

The following two charts illustrate in generalized terms the contrasting orientations, philosophies, and styles of the two major leadership functions of the house group movement. The first identifies the major contrasts, using phrases as frames of reference to highlight the differing principles of authority, structure, and function in the two systems. The second diagram contrasts how the chain of command works in each system, using terms which seem most appropriate to indicate the nature of the authority principle as it passes through the various levels of leadership.

Contrasting Authority Systems
of Major House Groups

(Generalized Principles)

The Supervision Paradigm	*The Submission Paradigm*
Chain of command through supervision	Chain of command through submission
Authority *through* the leader	Authority *in* the leader
Loyalty to the group and its cause	Loyalty to the leader
Community through a common purpose	Community through pyramidal interpersonal relations

The corporation model	The monastic model
Administrative hierarchy	Religious hierarchy
Functional orientation	Relational orientation
Fraternal relations	Paternal relations
Priesthood of the believer	Sacerdotalism
Common servanthood	Master-servant relationship
Democratic	Oligarchic
Congregational	Episcopalian
Directly evangelistic	Indirectly evangelistic
Institutional augmenting	Counterinstitutional

An Evaluation of Leadership and Authority Roles

Despite some weaknesses and negative aspects, the leadership roles of the house group phenomenon, like the movement itself, have many positive lessons from which the wider church can learn. Perhaps the strongest positive aspect of the movement is the recovery of the pastoral function in its most definitive meaning: disciplined caring.

Caring has, of course, been integral to the Christian movement from the beginning, and this aspect of the pastoral role has been evident from time to time all through Christian history. However, as churches have grown larger and larger in the wake of rapid Christian advancement in recent times, churches, like society itself, have become more and more impersonal. They have come to reflect, understandably, the bureaucratic model which increasingly has influenced all organizational forms in society, religious as well as secular.

What has been needed is the recovery of caring in a way which would touch peoples lives significantly. It is not enough to hear it from the pulpit, read it in the Bible, or see it in individuals. It has to be experienced in community. The house group movement has accomplished this. Here caring carries a profoundly disciplined character. Persons become responsible

Contrasting Chain of Command of Major Authority Systems of House Groups

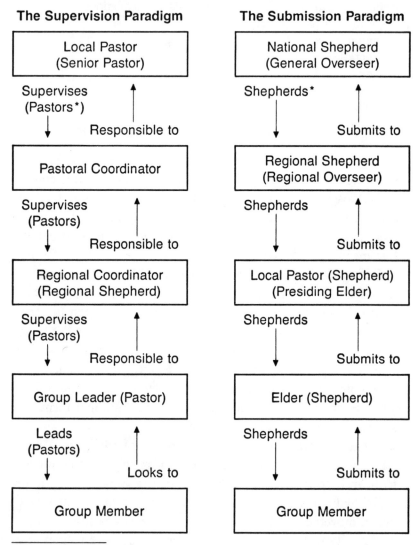

The Supervision Paradigm	The Submission Paradigm
Local Pastor (Senior Pastor)	National Shepherd (General Overseer)
Supervises (Pastors*) ↓ ↑ Responsible to	Shepherds* ↓ ↑ Submits to
Pastoral Coordinator	Regional Shepherd (Regional Overseer)
Supervises (Pastors) ↓ ↑ Responsible to	Shepherds ↓ ↑ Submits to
Regional Coordinator (Regional Shepherd)	Local Pastor (Shepherd) (Presiding Elder)
Supervises (Pastors) ↓ ↑ Responsible to	Shepherds ↓ ↑ Submits to
Group Leader (Pastor)	Elder (Shepherd)
Leads (Pastors) ↓ ↑ Looks to	Shepherds ↓ ↑ Submits to
Group Member	Group Member

*Note: read "Pastors" and "Shepherds" as verbs.

for certain other persons, and caring assumes a deeply meaningful relational aspect. If this has been carried too far, perhaps previous neglect has mandated the swinging of the pendulum back a bit far in order to compensate.

Another weakness in traditional church life, which the house group movement has endeavored to correct, has been the lack of church discipline and the vast numbers of nominal church members for whom the Christian faith has not been a truly vital force. The high level of commitment which the leadership of the movement has been able to inspire has served as an indictment of the traditional life of our churches.

The mobilization of the laity, which must constitute one of the highest priorities in the future mission strategy in our emerging urban world, has been a hallmark of this movement. The use of laypersons at various levels of leadership and the spiritual development of Christians in the house groups have helped to recover the lay atmosphere of the Christian movement reminiscent of the early Christian centuries.

From a methodological as well as theological perspective, the movement has shattered stereotypes of leadership development. It has been able to demonstrate that leadership can be developed more quickly, more soundly, and from more unlikely subjects than has been the norm in the past.

The effective leadership role of women, both at the administrative and house group level, has not only helped us to recover something we have missed from our New Testament heritage, it has demonstrated the unusual potential for numerical and spiritual growth which our churches could enjoy in the future. Not all house group ministries demonstrate this—indeed some would have an aversion to it—but such groups as the Yoido Full Gospel Church have dramatized the amazing leadership potential of women in ministry.

As positive as the overall development of leadership has been, however, there are some areas of concern. Perhaps no one area has evoked more concern in responsible Christian circles than the concept of submission. It is easy to understand the shepherding movement (and the Jesus movement) as a reaction to the irresponsible attitude and promiscuous style of the counterculture of the late sixties and early seventies. Yet there still persists great concern over the movement. It is not the purpose of this chapter to make an in-depth critique of the shepherding movement, as such, but to try to speak to this concern as it relates to our interest in the significance of the leadership function in house group movements, especially at the point of the authority principle. The motivation behind this authority principle seems to be one of caring, which is as genuine as it is among the other house group movements. Moreover, it is not so much the control in the system (which is designed to build in responsibility and accountability) as it is in the nature and extent of the control.

One line of thought will illustrate the problem. In chapter 6, Keith Curlee, pastor of the Houston Covenant Church, in explaining the relationship between one who submits himself to another and the one to whom he submits himself, commented that the teacher-learner relationship must not be seen in its Western connotation but in its first-century Middle-Eastern meaning:

> The word "disciple" has connotations of master and servant—what we would Westernize as teacher and class. (The master-servant relationship) has tremendous "governmental" force in a man's life; it shapes a person's life.[8]

It is understandable that the shepherding movement would seek scriptural support for its system. However, its interpretation of certain Scriptures reveals a basic misunderstanding of the New Testament. Understanding what may have been the Middle-Eastern mind-set is one thing, but the crucial point at issue is the teaching of the New Testament.

It is true that the cultural context must be understood (both the New Testament's and ours). This is a fundamental concept of contemporary missiology. However, while we acknowledge the value of insights from anthropology which have provided the principle of "Christ through culture," we appeal always ultimately to the theological principle of "Christ above culture." It is precisely on this subject that Jesus gave some of His clearest teachings on the subject of the master-servant situation in leadership. In fact, this very concept which prevailed in His world, He rejected. He said:

> Ye know that the princes of the Gentiles exercise dominion over them, and they that are great exercise authority upon them. But it shall not be so among you: but whosoever will be great among you, let him be your minister; And whosoever will be chief among you, let him be your servant (Matt. 20:25-27).

It is indisputably clear that Jesus warned against leaders assuming a master role over their followers. His clear teaching is that the leaders are to be servants. In fact, the uniquely Christian principle that true leadership is found in servanthood is distinct from the prevailing first-century Middle-Eastern view which Jesus condemned as Gentile (heathen, unbelieving) that leadership is mastery. Although a responsible and disciplined caring relationship may be intended, when this reversal of the New Testament mandate is structured, there can be potential danger in such a relational arrangement. It is not just the extent of the control itself which may eventuate into an unintended legalism but the nature of the control which may produce undue spiritual and psychological dependency, especially if it is perceived as being biblical.

Even though it is not intended—the more positive aspects of the shepherding movement indicate this—some responsible critics within the church can see tendencies which could be like, on the one hand, the classical sacerdotalism which developed in the Roman Catholic Church and, on the other hand, the extreme social control mechanisms employed by some modern cult groups. There is too much which is positive and constructive in the movement to let this happen, and we hope its solid evangelical moorings will be a corrective toward any tendency to go too far in the wrong direction.

Despite the above warning, we affirm the positive and inspiring developments in leadership roles seen in house churches, cell groups, and other types of Christian house groups. We are indebted to the new leaders for their serving as role models who have inspired a new generation of Christian dedication. We are grateful for their exciting and stimulating ideas which have helped us to recover much of our biblical heritage. We are challenged by the encouraging models of leadership which have been developed under their general oversight and creativity in the various house group phenomena. Most of all, we acknowledge and celebrate the recovery of much of the heart and soul of our faith which has come in the wake of this new leadership.

Notes

1. Walter J. Hollenweger, "The House Church Movement in Great Britain," *The Expository Time*, 86 (1982), pp. 45-47.

2. This quotation is attributed to J. E. E. Dalberg (Lord) Acton in a letter to Bishop Mandell Creighton dated April 3, 1887.

3. Paul Yonggi Cho, "Reaching Cities with Home Cells," *Urban Mission,* Jan. 1984, pp. 4-14.

4. Ibid., pp. 9–10.

5. Ibid., p. 10.

6. Cho, *Successful Home Cell Groups,* p. 51.

7. Cho, "Reaching Cities with Home Cells," pp. 5-7.

8. See chapter 6, p. 154.

9
Structure, Tradition, and Organizational Change

The house church and the home cell group are both forms of organizational innovation. As such, they are not seen as normal in this society, nor are they supported by existing traditional structures. They are relatively new forms which are introduced by cultural innovators who attempt to bridge the gap between unsatisfied needs and inflexible institutions. In some cases, these innovations are conducted entirely outside traditional bounderies while in other instances they occur within existing institutions, typically as efforts to revitalize rather than reject such organizations.

The house church as a form of church structure has the problem that it is not only seen as unorthodox, but it also tends to be rather unstable. Thus, those who would worship in this manner struggle not only to have others accept the form as legitimate, they also must counter the tendency of those within the house church movement who seek stability through greater structure. Over time, new or innovative groups have a natural tendency towards institutionalization: they seek stability through structure and cultural conformity.

Consequently, if a house church movement is successful in forming large numbers of churches, it is quite possible that the resulting congregations will eventually resemble conventional

218

churches, meeting in their own church buildings and accommodating middle-class culture. In short, they become no different from what they sought to replace.

The home cell group, on the other hand, is a more limited innovation which may be added to the structure of existing institutionalized churches rather than replacing them with a new form of church. In this sense the home cell group may be seen as less of a threat to mainline churches, and, in fact, we have seen many very conservative pastors embrace the concept with little hesitation. Opposition tends to come from entrenched organizations within the churches which may feel threatened by the new form. They ask, "Is it necessary? Doesn't Sunday School perform the same functions?"

Can either of these two forms succeed in American society? They already exist, of course, but can they become widespread and part of the everyday fabric of this culture? These are the same questions which are asked about every social movement, whether its goals are to overthrow the existing social order, to create a new religion, or to achieve something far more modest. House churches and home cell groups, if accepted, will not produce immediate revolutionary changes in the shape of American religion. But like the Sunday School movement of an earlier day, the subtle changes may be no less profound.[1]

The House Church: Resisting Institutionalization

The local Christian church began as a house church. As seen in an earlier chapter, however, it did not remain in this form for long once oppression was removed. Its evolution at this early date was not, of course, due to pressures to become like existing institutional church forms, since no such forms currently existed. Instead, the very success of the church—its increasing power and affluence and its need for stability, order, and control—led to the eventual displacement of the house church with the basilica.

In the years since the third century, house church movements have emerged from time to time for a variety of reasons. Chief among these has been to avoid persecution. In many periods of history, Christian groups were forced underground in order to worship as they saw fit. The second major reason for the rise of house churches is also attributable to religious dissent, though in this case a matter of choice: Christians have chosen the house church as a more authentic form of church structure. Finally, in recent years we have seen the house church promoted because of cost. Starting house churches is less expensive than more traditional methods of church planting.

All house church groups face the dilemma of institutionalization in that strong forces are operative which tend to move them in the direction of cultural accommodation. How these forces operate, however, differs according to which of the motivating factors led to the initial organization of the group.

Accommodation Following Coercion

The house churches in China are presently facing the dilemma of accommodation and institutionalization in a different guise than house churches in the United States. As we have learned, these house churches were formed primarily because of persecution. Until very recently, all churches were banned, even those which had formerly supported the state. Now, however, open churches are once again becoming legal, and Christians are facing pressures to abandon house churches in favor of the new open Three-Self churches.

Obviously, the Chinese church has thrived in its decentralized, reticulated form, and we presume that many feel that the house church structure is an advantage. If nothing else, it is the form in which the Chinese church has had its greatest growth.

It may well be, however, that most Christians in China would prefer to meet openly in church buildings. And if this is so, there is undoubtedly some temptation to accommodate with the state and join the open churches. To accommodate in China implies state control and supervision, and whether open worship is worth the price of government supervision is a question that millions of Chinese Christians must now address.

This is the dilemma that any "outlaw" house church movement faces once it "wins" (as did the third-century church), or is exiled to a context where its members rule, or when it becomes an acceptable alternative form of religious expression. There is a tendency eventually to leave behind the informal house church structure in each case.

Adaptation Without Accommodation

For the Houston Covenant Church, the Church of the Open Door in Los Angeles, several San Francisco Bay area house church ministries, and many other groups with roots in the Jesus movement, the primary motivation for starting house churches was not cost or to evangelize a specific unchurched population. The main goal was to intensify commitment among believers and pursue a more intimate form of worship. These groups developed both a community and an ideology which viewed the house church as an authentic church structure with a form of worship which had clear advantages over traditional mainline churches. This ideology gave such ministries a reason for remaining house churches, a quality that many other house church movements lacked.

Commitment to a form of worship was the key to the survival of these "counterinstitutional" house church groups, but it has not totally insulated them from pressures towards greater institutionalization. According to Max Weber, an authority structure founded on the charismatic personality of a leader cannot remain stable. In a real sense, in fact, this type of authority structure only exists as the movement is forming. Once in place, the house church movement, or any other movement which is beginning to become an established part of society, must begin to change in order to achieve a permanent routine structure.[2]

Based on Weber's insights into the dynamics of charisma and institution building, we can outline some probable outcomes for house churches. At the most basic level, a home fellowship group may begin the process of becoming permanent by organizing as a house church. The leader becomes pastor, and those who were participants become members. At the same time a fiscal organization comes into being to support the ministries of the group, the pastor, and his or her administrative staff. Essentially, the house church may become a formal organization, a small bureaucracy, where the leader occupies the bureaucratic position of pastor. Authority is thus transferred from the person of the leader to the position of the pastor.

The organizational impulse for security, which is a sociological constant, tends to move the house church movement toward greater levels of structure. The pressures grow especially intense if the movement experiences much growth. Increasingly, house churches require routine measures of communication to replace the informal guidance of the senior pastor. Training of leadership becomes essential. Eventually, this may lead to a Bible institute, seminary, or an ongoing series of training seminars. Administration may be such a problem that the leader's duties become largely confined to overseeing a group of house church pastors—he or she no longer personally oversees any of the house churches. In a sense, the leader has become an administrative head of a small denomination.

Again, according to Weber, there is "the objective necessity of adaptation of the patterns of order and of the organization of the administrative staff to the normal everyday needs and conditions of carrying on administration."[3] Positions are created, policies outlined, budgets adopted, and computers purchased. In short, the collection of informal house churches becomes a complex institution.

Of course, the process of institutionalization varies considerably in speed and degree, and its path is greatly influenced by the social context and the nature of the leader and the movement. But it would be safe to assume a definite tendency toward institution building as a necessary condition for long-term survival.

The easy answer to all the administrative pressures faced by the house church would be to purchase church buildings to house worship services, staff, committee meetings, secretaries, and the routine business of producing literature, processing contributions, and keeping in touch with members. This is exactly the step taken by one former house church in San Francisco. They purchased a school and are no longer a true house church. They are attempting to keep their worship services informal and as close to their former worship in homes as they can, but the change is already evident.

In the Houston Covenant Church, the commitment to home worship was such that instead of building churches for each of their congregations, a central office facility was constructed where all of the house church leaders could deal with administrative needs. This was a unique and effective way of dealing with the need for structure but avoiding compromising the group's commitment to house church worship. An equally effective step taken by the Houston Covenant Church was to arrange for the house churches to meet in the homes of the leaders. Their homes are purchased with this use in mind, with at least one very large room in which the house church can meet.

The example of the Houston Covenent Church suggests that even the accommodations to institutionalization can be innovative. The pressures which make greater structure necessary do not evaporate over time, and a movement must either resolve them or expect some future crisis will lead to dissolution. The easiest direction for a movement to go, of course, is to accommodate itself fully to the culture and simply imitate conventional practices. To establish and maintain an innovative religious organization is much more difficult. Careful decisions must be made in order to achieve a measure of stability, to deal with administrative needs, and to create a structure which can effectively cope with the outside world and yet retain those features which make it different.

Unfortunately for the continued survival of most house church groups, the commitment to their form of worship is not sufficiently strong to resist pressures which push them toward accommodation. House church movements are especially vulnerable to cultural accommodation because they are trying to maintain and promote an informal structure rather than create a new formal pattern of structure.

Despite this problem, we must keep in mind that new social or religious movements often heavily impact the traditional structures in the larger society even when they "fail." It is quite plausible that while these "protestant" fractions may not replace traditional churches, they may force a sorely needed reexamination of traditional church methods, including some redefinition of how church should be done. The measure of impact made by the movement must be judged by this effect as well as the success or failure of the organized house church movements.

Low-Cost House Churches

Innovative denominational agencies, like the Home Mission Board of the Southern Baptist Convention, recognized early on that the house church had certain advantages which could make it quite useful as a tool for evangelism. Two factors stood out as important. First, the many nondenominational house churches which were emerging out of the Jesus movement were attracting people who would never set foot in a traditional Baptist church. It was reasoned that by starting house churches of their own, Southern Baptists could begin to minister to a large unchurched population which had previously remained out of their reach.

A second reason for denominational involvement in starting house churches was simply their low cost. One of the major barriers to starting any new work is the high cost of real estate and the construction of church buildings. In major cities, this is a particularly difficult problem. The use of home Bible studies and rented facilities in such circumstances has been used for years, but the form had always been viewed as temporary. It was always implied that a "real church" needed permanent facilities which they owned.

As an experiment, the Home Mission Board employed church planters to begin house churches which would remain house churches, rather than encouraging the purchase of property at the earliest possible date. In this way the church could afford to employ a full-time pastor much sooner without the burden of a large mortgage. Also, the church could be involved in starting new house churches which could evangelize more people and sustain a larger volume of mission activity. The plan seemed promising, and church planters were sent on the field with the directive to begin house churches exclusively. They were even under threat of losing support if the churches they started purchased property.

The design did not work as planned. Even though people were attracted who would not have come to an institutionalized church, as soon as the house church became viable, its members began to want to purchase land and construct church buildings. So universal was this scenario that the program was finally abandoned. The Home Mission Board returned to encouraging home Bible studies which would eventually evolve into typically structured churches with property.

The failure of this attempt to start permanent house churches resulted from several factors. First of all, the people who were reached through this ministry were not committed to the house church as the best form of worship. The Home Mission Board intended for these groups to remain house churches, but the desire was not shared by the various participants. Without this commitment it was unlikely that the members would resist the various practical and cultural factors which moved them in the direction of becoming an institutionalized church with property. But why? Since the people recruited were evidently not attracted to the conventional trappings of mainline churches, why should they begin to gravitate toward them in structure?

At a basic level, the structure of these house churches implied impermanence. Understandably, people were afraid that one day the house church would simply dissolve. The limited resources of the groups prevented them from employing full-time pastors, which further added to their fears. Some groups became psychologically dependent upon their church planter. Yet it was known that these men would eventually leave. Therefore, the calling of a full-time "permanent" pastor and the construction of a building symbolized both security and stability. Whatever compromises were made in abandoning house church worship were felt to be offset by the alleviation of a precarious future.

Another major factor which undoubtedly influenced the direction of the HMB house churches was the type of leadership used. Rather than selecting or recruiting the charismatic individual who possessed a dynamic personality and compelling vision, the house churches were led by ordinary church planters who were following the directives of a denominational agency. Without a charismatic leader and a well-developed ideology, there was little sense among the members that they had been brought together by God for a special purpose, that their lives were being interwoven in a unique and complementary manner. They were simply a church which met in a home because it was less expensive, less threatening to non-Christians, and because their leader's supervisors thought they should continue to do so. This was not enough of a group incentive to sustain a house church.

A further problem was in the members' perception of their church. They had been influenced by a culture which viewed house churches as Bible studies rather than real churches. How did one respond when asked: "Where do you go to church?" When members were "unchurched," the home meetings seemed attractive, but now that they had joined and were no longer outsiders, cultural definitions of what a church should be affected their view of the house church. It now seemed too casual, too impermanent.

There were, of course, the unanticipated problems of a more practical nature as well. The strategy of the HMB was to use family-owned dwellings, for the most part. But this particular type of house church structure puts demands upon the host family. It was found that few people wanted to lodge an ongoing church in their homes, and the burden was disproportionately placed upon those families who had adequate accommodations. There was also a recurrent problem with finding satisfactory arrangements for the children.

Zoning restrictions have prompted more than a few large house church meetings to disband because of complaints by neighbors to the police. Though small meetings might be ignored or go unnoticed by community residents, the larger groups run a higher risk of objections by neighbors. In addition, cultural definitions of churches as buildings lead some residents to misconstrue the purpose of such groups, generating gossip and rumor about cults. While these cultural definitions have no biblical foundations, they still serve to stigmatize innovative efforts and reinforce conventional religious practices.

An individual house church may not have experienced all of the problems catalogued above, but it is virtually certain that many were felt. Each provided a push in the direction of purchasing property, building a building, and ceasing to be a house church. For churches without an ideology which makes the house church structure legitimate and without a charismatic leader to organize the churches into a movement, the evolution away from the house church is apt to be rapid. As soon as enough growth occurs and space becomes a problem, grumblings may turn quickly into a property committee.

The Home Cell Group: Conflict With Tradition

Home cell group ministries face a dilemma in America which is quite different from that confronting the house church. Instead of trying to resist the many pressures toward institutionalization, the home cell group faces conflict from the forces of tradition which see it as unnecessary. This was clearly seen in the case of Hoffmantown Baptist Church, and we have observed the same problem nearly every time an older church begins a home cell group ministry. The result of such conflict, however, does not have to be the de-emphasis of the home cell group ministry as it did at Hoffmantown. Many examples exist of churches which have successfully dealt with this problem. Still, the crisis which emerges is typically an acute one and must be faced by all churches which seek to add home groups to the existing structure of an older church.

The closest historical parallel to the conflict aroused by the home cell group movement in the United States today is that of the Sunday School movement in the late nineteenth and early twentieth century. The similarities are quite profound. Prior to this movement, established churches had only worship services. Any teaching which took place was either part of a sermon or occurred informally in homes. This relative lack of systematic Bible teaching was a need in search of a solution. As we well know today, that solution was the Sunday School.

Today we accept Sunday School as an integral part of the church. It has become a fixed tradition in our churches. At one time, however, Sunday School was a controversial and unorthodox innovation. At the time of its introduction it was seen as novel, unnecessary by many, and even radical by more than a few. Acceptance of Sunday School by Baptists and other denominations was largely the result of a major movement: the Sunday School movement. Reformers advocating the Sunday School labored feverishly across the nation publishing pamphlets, persuading skeptics, and preaching in churches. Sunday School societies were organized, and much resistance was encountered.[4] The result as we know now was success. Sunday School is well accepted in most of the United States, even though in some denominations Sunday Schools are seen as being for children only. A retrospective glimpse at the resistence surrounding the reception and endorsement of Sunday School provides an important insight. History is replete with innovations that initially are met with opposition before becoming cherished institutions.

The Sunday School movement began because of a need for Bible teaching. In a similar manner many church leaders have become concerned about the lack of spiritual nurture in our churches. Where are personal concerns expressed? Where does true fellowship and *koinonia* occur? Where are the structures that provide for the construction and maintenance of deep interpersonal relationships? Why do many churches resemble businesses rather than families? Where can church members expose their friends to Christian love when those friends will not come to church? Many feel that the traditional church and its programs provide these opportunities on a haphazard basis at best.

Some fellowship occurs in Sunday School or after the worship hour, but the time is too brief, and many are left out. Prayer concerns are voiced at Sunday School and at midweek prayer meetings, but often only those that are "safe" to express —primarily about illnesses. Very rarely do we hear prayers for unsaved persons or about personal problems or even about job losses and other financial crises. There should be somewhere that such needs are addressed on an ongoing basis and where those who are usually left out are included and loved.

Even with the obvious need for a ministry like the home cell group, resistance is still inevitable. Traditional organizations do not undergo substantial change without some resistance and conflict. In the case of well-established churches which have tried to add the home cell group to an existing array of ministries, conflict has generally come from older members and particularly from those who see the groups as threatening the Sunday School. To some extent these fears have been well founded because, in the initial enthusiasm to start home cell groups, some teachers have felt their gifts could be better used leading one of the cell groups than teaching the Sunday School. This has led to some competition for leaders.

Perhaps more seriously, some pastors feel that to achieve the growth of Korean models a church might actually need to abolish Sunday School, adding its teaching function to the home cell groups. This "territorial" conflict can be a serious one as we observed in chapter 5.

There would, however, appear to be no organizational reason why Sunday School would have to be abandoned. The function of home cell groups can complement other ministries of the church. With regard to the limited supply of leaders, the cell groups should not create a problem since they basically depend on self-generated leadership. The notion that these two church structures must be mutually exclusive is erroneous. Indeed, as cell groups grow, they can actually create an influx of new members into a Sunday School program. Many observers have misunderstood the reasons underlying the particular characteristics of the Korean model. The reason that the largest Korean churches have no Sunday School is the lack of a strong tradition of Sunday School in their denominations rather than an inherent conflict between home cell groups and Sunday School. To prove our point that no necessary conflict exists, we need only to point to the largest Baptist churches in Seoul which have both cell groups and Sunday School.

Cultural Transfer

The significance of the home cell group is occasionally discounted by some who feel that it is a cultural form more suited to Korea than to the United States or other Western nations. On this basis, it is usually held that no church in the West will ever grow to the size of the Yoido Full Gospel Church, and the home cell group is little more than a passing fad—like the Jesus movement and its "Christian houses."

However, the massive growth of a single church is not imperative to the success or effectiveness of the home cell movement. Growth can be diffused through many churches and have an equally impressive impact. Perhaps the most serious objection one hears is that the success of the cell model in the Orient is predicated upon the authoritarian nature of Korean culture. This objection deserves some comment.

Korean culture may tend to encourage group harmony over individualism, and this tendency along with a history of authoritarian political leadership may indeed support the development of larger informal organizations than could be expected in the United States. This theory, however, has not been tested and may be only of limited value in explaining why similar growth patterns do not exist as yet in the United States. It should be remembered that the massive growth seen among several churches in Seoul resulted primarily from the cultural innovation of home cell groups rather than a religious form with roots in traditional Korean culture. Cho, as an authoritarian leader, might have been expected to impose this new form on his church with little opposition from a supposedly docile Korean congregation. As we have seen, however, this did not occur. He received substantial opposition from the leaders of the church and had to turn to persons with little influence within the congregation in order to obtain cell-group leaders. The initial meetings were not attended by large numbers, and the effort could have failed at any time in this early period.[5]

What saved the home cell groups in Korea is the same thing which could lead to their predominance in the United States: functionality. Acceptance came especially quickly in Korea because of the pressing need for such groups in the absence of Sunday School and because of the relative newness of Christianity and organized church life in Korea. Traditions had not been as firmly established as they were in the United States. For this reason, innovations were judged more on the basis of their benefit than on their conventionality.

The primary obstacle to home cell groups in the United States is not adapting them to Western culture but in overcoming the resistance to innovation by a very tradition-bound institution. To be sure, some adaptation is necessary, and it would be foolish to try to transfer the concept totally intact from a Pentecostal church in Seoul, Korea, to a staid Baptist church in Richmond, Virginia. Churches in the United States do not have to dissolve Sunday School merely in order to emulate the Yoido Full Gospel Church. This would only perpetuate their flaw. The most serious indictment of American churches is that they have not dealt effectively with the need for *koinonia* and their unwillingness to accept a programatic innovation which can effectively deal with the need.

Institutional Obstacles

For the home cell group movement to succeed in the manner of the Sunday School movement, several institutional obstacles need to be overcome. The first is the recognition of a need for the function provided by the home cell groups. The second is the development of legitimacy of the innovation; and the third is the integration of the cell groups into existing church structure.

Critics maintain that the functions of home cell groups are provided by other church programs, and there is no need to add a new program. This view is more of an affirmation of the past than a valid reason for rejecting home cell groups. If in fact they were needed, churches would have had them long ago, or so the argument goes. A little reflection, however, or a conversation with a few pastors about the spiritual maturity of their members should be enough to dispel such criticism. In fact, it has been the pressing need for *koinonia*, for intercessory prayer, for mutual support, and for a place in which all members can feel wanted and loved that has motivated pastors all over the United States to begin home cell ministries.

This rationale is more often given than that of growth. Evangelical pastors want the growth they see in the Yoido Full Gospel Church, but what prompts the urgency to start home cell groups is more often the acute awareness of an unmet need within their flock. This urgency, however, must also be felt by the lay leadership of a church for such a program to get off the ground. Too often a pastor will try to begin without this full support. Some can pull it off, but many have not achieved the combination of trust and power to do so. The safest strategy, and the one more likely to succeed, is for a pastor first to convince his key leadership of the need, especially those with responsibility over the Sunday School, before proceeding. Ownership and a shared awareness of need are essential.

Legitimacy for a new program can come from many sources. In some cases the acceptance of the pastor is enough. His charismatic leadership and the trust of his members provide legitimacy for any program which is proposed. This is not often the case, even for "superchurches" with very influential leaders.

Legitimacy can also be provided by the example of other respected churches within a denomination. "If they are doing it, it must be OK." This is the reason the current experiments by First Baptist, Atlanta; First Baptist, Dallas; Second Baptist, Houston; and Bellevue Baptist, Memphis, are so significant in the Southern Baptist Convention. If they succeed, the form will gain an almost instant legitimacy among conservative churches in the Southern Baptist Convention. If they fail to do so, however, or if the programs are canceled because of internal conflict, the legitimacy of home cell groups as a viable new form could be heavily damaged.

Another possible source of legitimacy for home cell groups is through their acceptance by major denominational agencies. Denominational agencies such as The Sunday School Board of the Southern Baptist Convention, the Board of Discipleship of the United Methodist Church, or the Support Agency of the Presbyerian Church USA could lend substantial credibility to home cell group programs. For instance, major steps could be taken toward this end by providing literature to inform and clarify functions, specify goals, and support could be offered by way of assistance and consultation in organizing the groups. Further legitimacy might be achieved through symposiums or thematic sessions at national, regional, or state conventions.

Even with legitimacy provided at the denominational level and by respected churches, any church which begins a home cell group ministry can expect some problems in integrating the new form into existing church organization. Issues will emerge concerning leadership of the groups, training, the formulation of curriculum (if there is to be teaching), and conflict with Sunday School or other church programs.

We reiterate our earlier points regarding strategy: initiating the process with a great deal of careful preparation, taking advantage of consultants if they are available, acquiring support from lay leaders, working toward a corporate attitude of ownership, and providing a well-developed theology of home cell groups and their functions.

In the next chapter we deal more specifically with how to set up house churches and home cell groups and how some of the major organizational problems can be either avoided or solved.

Notes

1. See Lynn E. May, *A Brief History of Southern Baptist Sunday School Work* (unpublished manuscript, 1964), p. 6. Also see Henry F. Cope, *The Evolution of the Sunday School* (Boston: The Pilgrim Press, 1911).

2. Max Weber, "Bureaucracy," *The Sociology of Organizations,* eds. Oscar Grusky and George Miller (New York: The Free Press, 1970), pp. 5-24. Also see Max Weber, *Max Weber on Charisma and Institution Building,* S.N. Eisenstadt (ed)., (Chicago: University of Chicago Press), p. 19.

3. Ibid. pp. 21-22.

4. May, pp. 6-25.

5. Paul Y. Cho, *Successful Home Cell Groups* (Plainsfield: N.J.: Logos International, 1931), p. 22.

10
Models for Denominational Involvement

The church is a dynamic institution which has evolved continuously since its beginning nearly two millennia ago. Over the centuries many structural forms of church have emerged, and this variety should not be surprising. Churches are social institutions which must exist and attempt to thrive in a variety of cultural contexts. As such, they have adapted to political and social settings, to differing environments and cultures, to repression and freedom, to affluence and poverty, to power and weakness, to good theology and heresy. All have affected how we worship and the structure of what we call a local church.

The many forms of church structure visible now and throughout Christian history may be seen as a flaw or as a sign of healthy diversity. We hold the latter view because the Bible offers relatively few guidelines concerning how churches should be organized. What we see instead in the Scriptures are tantalizing glimpses of first-century worship with advice about how to resolve problems which arose. Jesus said nothing about local church structure, and even the apostle Paul said very little that can be taken to imply that churches should be organized in any particular manner. An honest reading of the New Testament and the writings of the church fathers reveals that the church began as a loosely organized movement in which highly structured local churches as we know them did not exist.

The Christian movement evolved from an unstructured mass movement to unified collections of home meetings to a hierarchical network of local churches. It changed in necessary reaction to its growth, to the culture, to persecution, to new theological understanding, and to the needs of its people. The church has continued to change in reaction to these same forces.

House churches and home cell groups have emerged in the present era largely because of need. Just as the church changed in the first century to adjust to growth and persecution, the church today must adjust to the loss of community. This is a need which has long faced mainline churches, but in recent years it has become more acute because of the increasing pervasiveness of shallow secondary relationships. We know people, but we do not really know them.

A grass-roots backlash has begun in modern societies resulting in greater and greater emphasis being placed on creating new structures where close primary relationships are able to flourish. Home-related worship is part of this larger trend. Members are no longer satisfied with their church being another impersonal institution. Either the church will provide them with structures conducive to primary relationships and true *koinonia,* or they will start their own.

Christian house groups are adaptations to a cultural problem and to a flaw in mainline churches. The need for community, for love, trust, and mutual concern among Christians has long existed. Now, however, that need has become urgent because of changes in modern society. A complex movement has emerged which has broken free from its initial causes: it now has a life of its own. The movement has many faces and many problems. It must be refined and managed, and if this can be done, the modern church will be infused with new life.

The House Church:
Advantages and Potential Disadvantages

Advantages

The house church, as a form of church structure, has many strong points, and a number of potential weaknesses as well. These are outlined in table 1. From a church-planting perspective, a distinct advantage of the house church over many other forms is its relatively low cost. Since house churches meet in homes, there is no need to buy property, build a building, pay mortgage notes, and deal with massive heating, cooling, and maintenance costs. This frees funds for pastoral support, mission efforts, and ministry. The house church may be the only way a denomination can afford to start new churches in cities where property costs are very high.

In addition to cost, an advantage of the house church is seen in the efficient use and development of leaders. The small ratio of leader to members makes true pastoring possible. The house church pastor, with few in his flock, can easily know, love, counsel, and guide each member—something that is not feasible in a large traditional church. The house church tends to put a primary emphasis on the pastoral role and on the development of new leaders from among the membership. In addition, laypersons are used very effectively to help lead the house church. The overdependence on paid, ordained clergy is not likely to be found here.

Of all the attractive elements exhibited by house churches, perhaps the most important is the quality of group life. This includes informal fellowship and relationships that exist among

Table 1

Advantages and Potential Disadvantages
of the House Church

Advantages	Potential Disadvantages
1. Low cost	1. Instability
2. Efficient use and development of lay leaders	2. Theological drift
	3. Abuse of authority
3. Quality of group life (Strong orientation toward mutual responsibility and commitment)	4. Control of meetings
4. Inclusive nature	
5. Growth potential (Greater appeal to some segments of unchurched population)	

members as well as the "formal" worship services of the church. The smallness of the group and the home setting is conducive to the formation of close face-to-face relationships between members. These are encouraged as are the sharing and prayer over personal needs and concerns and expressions of love and mutual support. In this environment people feel known, loved, and tend to exhibit very high levels of personal commitment to the group.

Related to the quality of meetings is the inclusive nature of house churches. Since everyone knows one another well and a high level of commitment exists, there is very little possibility that a member could reduce participation or quit the fellowship without very intensive efforts being made to bring the individual back to full participation. No one "falls through the crack" as so often happens in large churches.

The inclusiveness of house churches is also apparent in the

tendency of such groups to accept "misfits" or persons with minor emotional problems. Rather than being homogeneous fellowships of young urban couples, house churches are often (but not always) heterogenous mixtures. Anyone who will attend, follow the rules, and participate is generally accepted and loved.

House churches have great growth potential. With such little structure, small monetary investment and size limitations, it is natural for house church groups to divide and redivide when they grow too large. This is not a split; it is a planned division which results in a multiplication of groups. Some groups, of course, are more interested in ministry to one another than in outreach, but for those which want to grow and which regularly train new leaders, great potential exists.

Potential Disadvantages

Along with all of its advantages, the house church also has a few problems. One of the more serious of these is the typically unstable nature of house churches. For those relatively uncommitted to the house church as an organizational form, the pull toward becoming a traditional church with property and a building is very strong. A building solves many organizational problems, and when a church can afford to buy, it generally will do so despite the natural changes which must occur in the character and quality of worship. This creates a serious problem for denominational programs to start house churches.

The basic problem of how to achieve stability and yet retain the house church nature is best addressed by the Houston Covenant Church. Commitment to home worship is not enough, nor is charismatic leadership, as evidenced by the transition to rented facilities for Sunday worship by several San-Francisco Bay-area house church ministries. Instead, a house church ministry must add certain structures which act as safe-guards against the drift away from being a true house church. Chief among these in the HCC was the purchasing of homes for the leaders with large areas for meetings, the decision always to hold group meetings in one location, and the action to build a central office for the group leaders for more efficient adminis-tration and communication. All of this assumes, of course, that the leadership is very committed to house church structure and has helped convince members that this structure is worth pre-serving.

Theological drift, or the tendency toward heresy, is another problem house churches often exhibit. In truth this is not a problem unique to house churches but is one common to any independent group which rejects dominant cultural patterns. A charismatic leader is often followed with unquestioning loyalty by the membership; and if such a leader begins to drift toward an odd doctrinal stance or even heresy, there is no one to check the tendency.

House church groups which begin with leaders soundly trained in theology, which do not put too much authority in the hands of their leaders, and which are part of a larger denomina-tion or collection of house churches are unlikely to suffer from theological drift.

The abuse of authority by house church leaders is a problem which causes many to fear house church ministries. This prob-lem has two dimensions. The first is the tendency of untrained or wrongly chosen leaders to become "little caesars," as one house church leader put it. Without the constraints of a congre-gational polity structure, an immature house church leader can become quite autocratic.

The second aspect of the authority problem is seen in the shepherding concept. While we believe that under ideal circumstances the idea of hierarchical submission may work in a non-coercive manner, there remain possibilities for abuse. Perhaps these can be held in check, perhaps not. From a different perspective, it can be argued that the overemphasis on authority and submission violates the New Testament imperative of the leader's primary role as a servant.

It is important, however, to remember that shepherding is not inherently connected with the house church. Instead, it is part of a particular house church group's ideology. House churches can easily be started with different ideologies.

A final set of problems which face all house church ministries is in the control of meetings. The informal nature of the house church setting lends itself to certain organizational problems not faced by traditional churches. First, there is the problem of where to meet. Some groups rotate the meeting site, which may cause communication and scheduling problems. Other groups only meet in the leader's home or at the home of a member who has a large living room. This is more efficient. Other problems include not being able to start on time, continuing too late, and the tendency of informal meetings to get off track. A fairly strong leader and a flexible, but set, order of service can solve most of these problems on a week-to-week basis. Lastly, there is the universal home-worship problem of what to do with children. Various solutions exist.

Our major point in this review of the advantages and potential disadvantages of house churches is that many advantages exist, and while the objections may seem formidable, many are based on inaccurate perceptions of the house church and the tendency to view all groups as similar in structure and ideology. The problems which do exist can and have been overcome by many house churches around the world. The house church is not for everyone, but it does have a contribution to make and should not be dismissed as unworkable or an invitation to heresy.

The Home Cell Group:
Advantages and Potential Disadvantages

Advantages

Like the house church, the key feature which makes the home cell group attractive is the quality of group life. We stressed througout the book that the traditional mainline church provides for worship and teaching in an adequate manner. Some churches are more formal than others, some emphasize emotion, some have "soul" while others lack it badly. In each case, however, an individual can experience satisfying worship as he or she desires to do so. Similarly, teaching in the form of Sunday school or church school is widely available, although some churches stress it more than others. Somehow, however, the need for nurture, *koinonia,* fellowship, expressions of mutual concern and love has been ignored. They occur, no doubt, but haphazardly, and many Christians are left out.

The home cell group provides a place where Christians can come to know and understand one another, not hurriedly during opening assembly prior to church school or semiformally during a postworship coffee fellowship. Instead, the development of close, caring, face-to-face relationships occurs naturally and intentionally in the comfortable setting of a member's home. As prayer concerns are expressed, as people pray, and as trust develops, casual relationships deepen and commitment to the group intensifies. It is a natural process which occurs easily in home cell groups.

The home cell group also makes efficient use of lay leaders. Even more than the house church, the home cell group uses lay

Table 2

Advantages and Potential Disadvantages
of the Home Cell Group

Advantages	Potential Disadvantages
1. Quality of group life (Strong orientation toward mutual responsibility and commitment) 2. Efficient use of lay leaders 3. Growth potential (a) Mechanism for neighborhood evangelism (b) Greater appeal initially to some segments of unchurched population	1. Conflict with traditional institutions of the church (Resistance to change, particularly among older members) 2. Control of meetings 3. Splintering 4. Theological drift

leaders to the fullest. In many home cell ministries, only the first two levels of leadership are performed by clergy. Typically, both the regional directors (or shepherds), and the actual home cell group leaders are laypersons. Cell group leaders are constantly looking for members to become leaders, and training takes place both within the group setting and at a more formal level by the pastoral coordinator or even the senior pastor. New leaders are essential to the growth of a home cell ministry in order that new cells can be established and the member-to-leader ratio kept small.

The home cell group has also led to a reemphasis on the role of pastor. People in cell groups have a pastor of their own in their cell leader. He or she knows them better than the senior pastor ever could, even if the church is small. Even if the group leader is not called pastor, he or she functions in that role and allows the senior pastor to extend himself far beyond his own limits to care for the many individuals that make up the congregation.

Growth potential is another reason why many churches have investigated home cell groups. The tremendous growth of the Yoido Full Gospel Church and other huge churches in Seoul, has led churches all over the world to hope that kind of growth can be duplicated. Whether a church in the United States can reach half a million in membership is not possible to know, but it seems clear that the cell group can give a church new growth potential.

First, if cell groups can avoid becoming closed-support groups and organize with evangelism in mind, they act as a funnel whereby those uncomfortable with the church can begin to worship in a nonthreatening setting. Alternatively, different types of cell groups can be established, some with the goal of *koinonia* for Christians, others with the primary goal of reaching and ministering to non-Christians. Ralph Neighbour's TOUCH-point groups are an example of the latter.

In addition to growing by tapping new populations which were formerly cut off from the church, home cell groups add the important dimension of exponential growth. If groups are designed to grow, divide, and grow again, with additional divisions each year, a church can nearly achieve exponential growth (at least for a while). For this to occur all cell groups must have the same goals (to grow and divide). The total number of groups in the church doubles as all groups divide, and it doubles again as the new groups grow and then divide. The increase in groups is small at first, but if the doubling can be sustained, the growth curve resembles the exponential function or J curve, so often seen in projections of world population. The Yoido Full Gospel Church is growing at close to this level.

Potential Disadvantages

Home cell groups have received relatively little of the harsh criticism that is often directed at house churches. Rather than replacing the church structures as we know them, home cell groups are viewed as an additional ministry or a new program which can be added to programs which already exist. Home cell groups do not threaten pastors, who often are the first to see the need for such ministries. Instead, they appear to threaten already-existing programs of the church. Conflict with traditional institutions of the church is the key problem faced by the home cell group movement.

In the mainline churches we have observed, conflict has surfaced for the following reasons: competition for leaders, lack of ownership and low participation by older members, the tendency of the pastor and other home cell group leaders to move too fast, the threat of abolishing Sunday School, a reduction in the perceived importance of Sunday School by church leaders, poor communication of home cell group goals, and general suspicion of new programs by tradition-minded members. Some conflict with traditional institutions in the church is to be expected, but serious problems can be avoided if the pastor is a strong leader with long tenure, if the program proceeds slowly in its planning stages, if Sunday School receives equal emphasis, if no plans are made to abolish Sunday Schools, if older members are included in the planning and administration of the groups, and if the positive results of the groups are communicated clearly and often by the pastor.

Above all, traditional institutions must not feel that they are being threatened—as clearly occurred at Hoffmantown Baptist in Albuquerque. Cell group leaders should not be trained during the Sunday School hour, and the separate functions of the home cell groups should be stressed. A clear case must be made that the groups and the Sunday School are complementary, not competitive, ministries.

A relatively minor problem experienced by cell groups is seen in the control of meetings. Informal meetings are always in danger of becoming too informal, and if this happens, nothing is accomplished and participants become frustrated. We believe that the groups need leaders to insure that meetings start and end on time and that a definite but relaxed order of service is followed. A leader is also needed to train new leaders to take over a new group when the meeting becomes too large.

It is possible for members to become so attached to their leaders and so excited about the cell group that they want to break away and form a house church. We call this the problem of *splintering*. Alternatively, a regional director may feel the host church is too tradition minded and unresponsive to the needs of the home cell ministry and may try to pull his or her groups out of the church. Both possibilities are unlikely and can be avoided by the proper selection of leaders and through good communication and supervision.

Finally, there is the rare problem of theological drift. As in the house church, there is the possibility of a cell group leader pursuing some theological tangent so far that it leads to doctrinal conflict with the host church.

Deviations of any major sort are unlikely in home cell groups, however, because, unlike house churches, they are closely tied to a host church. Leaders are trained and supervised by church leaders, and potential problems can be quickly spotted and resolved. Church leaders who are considering home cell ministries should take care to build into the ministry careful procedures for training, supervision, and accountability for leaders. A ministry of this sort cannot be started and "turned loose" and expected to develop in the manner intended by church leadership. Like any other program, planning and close supervision are essential.

Options for the Denominational House Church

It should be apparent that very few denominational house churches exist today. House churches have tended to form in reaction to persecution, as in China, or as a protest against the type of worship found in traditional churches. Since Christian churches are not persecuted in the United States, the primary examples of the house church are countercultural groups which generally have their roots in the so-called Jesus movement. These groups have formed partially in reaction against mainline denominational churches, making it extremely unlikely that they would see any need to affiliate with a denomination.

Despite the rarity of house churches which are connected with mainline denominations, we hold that starting them is quite feasible and is a strategy which should be pursued by denominational mission organizations. It can be a significant part of a larger effort to reach sectors of the population which would not otherwise be reached by traditional efforts at church planting.

New efforts at planting denominational house churches should take special note of the problems experienced by those formed through the efforts of the Southern Baptist Home Mission Board. As was seen in this experiment, starting the house churches was much easier than keeping them as house churches. There is a definite tendency for those who are not committed to the concept to seek property as soon as the church begins to crowd its host's home. For leaders trained in many mainline seminaries and for most Christians in America, the edifice complex is very strong.

The High-Rise House Church

In very large cities in the United States and around the world, many residents live in high-rise apartments, condominiums, and co-ops in or near the central business district. Such areas are generally severely unchurched, often with one or two small churches to serve thirty thousand or more residents. All too often, these churches are complacent older congregations with large endowments and with members who feel little need or desire to reach the many high-rise residents in their community. Eventually a denomination may be able to start a new church which will better match nearby residents using the facilities of one of these older congregations, but until this is possible there is little likelihood that a new traditional church with property and a building can be started. The cost of real estate is simply too high.

A viable alternative for a denominational mission organization in the above situation is to begin a house church in one of the high-rise developments in the area. This would normally involve funding a church planter, moving him or her to the city, and renting or purchasing an apartment. The church planter's home would serve as the facility for the new congregation. This individual would try to reach neighbors in the building or in other buildings in the area and invite them to worship at the house church (or home Bible study, in some cases). It is not necessary or even likely that members would all be drawn from one building.

Once a core congregation had been gathered, the church planter could begin the process of leadership training. An individual with leadership potential and some personal charisma could be asked to assist in leading the church and eventually trained to assume pastoral duties over the group. When the new leader was ready and when the church had grown large enough, it could divide.

Early in the development of a high-rise house church, its leader should begin the process of convincing members that the special nature of house church worship was worth preserving. In this case the leader is assisted by the fact that purchasing a building would be far too costly. But to avoid frustration over the inability to afford property, it is essential that the members become committed to remaining a house church, as has happened in the case of Baptist work in Singapore.

The ultimate goal of the high-rise house church is to form an interlocking network of house churches in many downtown apartment buildings. Some may reach the size and affluence necessary to hire at least a part-time pastor while others would rely on trained laypersons. Many persons could be reached through this strategy who would never attend one of the downtown cathedral-like structures. Beginning the process would certainly not be easy, but once the process was underway, it could develop into a local house church movement.[1]

Care would have to be exercised constantly to keep the groups tied to the denomination which started them. Early on, the churches should teach missions education, stewardship, and the strength in cooperative efforts at missions. And even though the house churches do not fit the typical denominational mold, their leaders should be treated as pastors and their congregations as true churches by other pastors and by local denominational officials.

The Base-Satellite Unit

As described in chapter 4, base-satellite units are mission-type house churches which are sponsored by a host church. They can also be viewed as a cross between the home cell group and the independent house church. The units are tied to a host church, yet each unit meets separately on Sunday morning, has its own pastor, budget, and officers.

The base-satellite unit appears to be a form of house church which denominational churches can start with relatively little risk and with great possibilities for growth. This should not be too surprising since this concept was developed by the Baptist General Convention of Texas as a strategy for developing new churches. This strategy is called the Indigenous Satellite Program in Texas and was devised in order to help churches reach the many small pockets of unreached persons in their communities.

The designers of this program recognized that nearly all Southern Baptist churches are quite homogeneous in race, ethnicity, and socioeconomic status and at the same time are literally surrounded by persons who will never attend because they are different. The designers also recognized that many persons are uncomfortable in the formal institutionalized church setting. In response, a plan was devised to develop small new churches in each of the under-evangelized pockets of a community.

Satellite units can be started cheaply in rented housing using laypersons from the host church as "seed families." Unlike traditional efforts at church planting, the units are not intended to separate organizationally from the host church as they grow but will instead remain part of the larger organization and divide once average attendance reaches around fifty persons. In this way the units will multiply in number, reaching into blue-collar enclaves, apartment complexes, trailer parks, and other hard-to-penetrate areas. Rather than ending up with a middle-class clone of itself, the mother church oversees the development of a local community force which touches many more persons and many more types of people than it could expect through its own efforts or through starting a new traditional church. The mother church, however, should communicate clearly at all times that any person in these satellite groups are welcome to become active members and an integral part of the mother church.

Problems with theological drift can be avoided through the supervision of the mother church. Paternalism must be avoided, of course, or the units may be driven away. This is one of the few risks in starting the units.

Detailed instructions for starting satellite units are provided in *The Indigenous Satellite Program Manual,* published by the Church Extension Section of the Baptist General Convention of Texas. To this manual, we would add a section which describes the advantages of small-group worship. Leaders should receive special training in small-group worship; and when they become pastors of units, an effort should be made to communicate the advantages of remaining small. Members of units may be willing to divide their unit (or multiply, as the manual recommends) in order to reach more people, but their enthusiasm will no doubt be greater if they personally benefit. Preserving the intimate character of worship, the warm caring fellowship and the face-to-face relationships are some of these benefits, and they need to be stressed.[2]

Mobilizing the House Church: Building a Local Movement Organization

The most challenging yet most potentially successful house church option for a denominational church or a mission agency is to attempt to build a local movement organization. This option is difficult because movements are not easily planned; religious movements typically emerge through the innovative leadership of one person whose charismatic personality and "dream" draws people to be followers. But it would be a mistake to ignore or underestimate the critical role of rational action and organizational planning in social movements. In recent years, researchers of social movements increasily have come to acknowledge the value of these previously underrated factors.[3]

Various strategies can be imagined in beginning a house church movement. We would recommend, however, that the initiating agency emulate the general organizational scheme developed by the Houston Covenant Church. This does not imply that a Baptist group must accept the shepherding ideology, only that the very effective organizational solutions to basic house church problems be adopted. Key among these is to have house church meetings at the home of the leader. This solves the problem of where to meet; and if the home is large enough, the group will have to grow substantially before it must divide. The HCC has also dealt effectively with the problem of children during worship by having younger members care for them.

House churches must be structured to remain house churches, or they tend to evolve into traditional churches and lose the audience for whom they were intended. When growth occurs, members must be committed enough to their form of worship to divide the group into two parts rather than to purchase a larger meeting place. And when administrative demands become great, the solution of the Houston Covenant Church to construct a central office building is a promising option because it dealt with a need without compromising the nature of the small-group process.

We would suggest that a movement strategy begin with one or two young families. A recent seminary graduate with a charismatic personality who is committed to the denomination, who really desires to work with small groups, and who may be slightly disenchanted with traditional church structure would be a good choice. Such a person may have had some background in the Jesus movement. A house would be provided for the pastor/house church planter which was large enough to house the meetings. A salary would also be necessary until the church grew large enough to provide support.

A community study would reveal areas of a city with large numbers of unchurched young adults. The pastor would buy or rent a house in one of these areas and begin the slow process of visiting residents, witnessing, and organizing a small group of persons who are attracted to home worship. If a church can provide several "seed families" to help in this process, all the better. The new group would likely begin as a home Bible study and eventually progress toward a house church, once the participants became committed to the concept.

After it had organized, the new house church would affiliate with the local denominational association of churches (session, presbytery, or other locally based judicatory). The pastor would participate in denominational meetings, and the church would contribute to the denomination's cooperative missions program. In this way the house church would remain tied to the larger denomination, members could see the advantages of cooperation, and the church would be less likely to drift into questionable doctrine or practice.

One house church does not make a movement, of course, and the pastor/house church planter should begin training a new house church leader very early. In some cases the pastor may be able to ask a seminary friend who has similar ideas about home worship to lead a new group, but more frequently a member of the original house church will be trained to assume this role. Unlike the original leader, the new leader will not be subsidized by the denomination. When the group divides, the new house church should have enough strength to provide at least partial support for their new pastor. The position may thus begin as bivocational, but as the church grows it should become full time.

As the house churches multiply in the fledgling movement, administrative needs will increase accordingly. The original leader must act as both a pastor and as the movement director. Eventually, this may lead to the need for a central office with the director giving up duties as a house church pastor.

Throughout the development of this type of movement, a major stress should be on the need for intimate worship, close fellowship, caring, and concern, all of which occur most naturally in the house church setting. Care must be taken not to criticize traditional churches too heavily lest members begin to feel no need to remain part of a denomination. The emphasis should be on the necessity of providing a form of worship for those uncomfortable with more formal churches. Members may feel that the house church is "better," but they should also be taught that other forms are legitimate.

The growth potential of a local house church movement is tremendous. It may be quite difficult to build, but this should not dissuade innovative missionaries and seminarians from attempting to do so. Many people will be reached, and the denomination may discover that there are many effective ways of organizing an urban church.

Options for Home Cell Groups

Home cell groups come in various shapes and sizes in the United States. Even though many have used the Yoido Full Gospel Church in Seoul, Korea, as a model, few have tried to duplicate the exact structure of its home cell group ministry.

Instead, churches in the United States have experimented and created new forms of worship in the home.

Some congregations have decided to emphasize nurture over growth. Others, fearing stagnation, dissolve cell groups if they do not grow and divide on their own within a year or two. Most cell groups include both teaching as well as other activities, but Bellevue Baptist Church in Memphis, Tennessee, decided not to include any Bible study or teaching, choosing instead to emphasize fellowship, nurture, prayer, and caring. Most cell groups have leaders, yet at least one author recommends that home cell groups be leaderless. Finally, most churches have their cell groups meet weekly, but in one Baptist church in Nashville, the cell groups (here called neighborhood groups) meet infrequently—as if church leaders felt the groups were worthwhile but not "safe" enough to use on a regular basis.

We have tried to look at the various options available to the denominational church interested in beginning a home cell group ministry. Our recommendations are divided into two sets: one for older churches and a second for new churches which are to be organized through a cell group ministry.

The Established Church and the Cell Group

Most churches are seeking to add a cell group ministry to an already-established program. To do so effectively, a church needs a clear rationale which can be communicated to gain support and silence potential detractors. And if possible, the impetus for the decision to begin such a ministry should come (or seem to come) from laypersons rather than from the pastor. The program must be "owned" by the membership and not seen as "that wild scheme which the pastor cooked up." The start-up should thus proceed very slowly.

The simplest rationale for the home cell group is to provide an organized means for fellowship, *koinonia,* intercessory prayer, mutual support, and caring. To this rationale can be added the growth potential of cell groups, and in combination these advantages will sway almost any long-range planning committee. The clear functional differences between cell groups and Sunday School should be underscored, so the defenders of traditional programs will not feel threatened.

Following the development of a rationale, a church should decide the type of cell group meetings it wishes to have. Many are possible. From our observations, we would recommend that cell groups have assigned leaders, that the groups meet once a week, and that they include a short Bible study along with other activities. This duplicates the function of Sunday School to a certain extent, but Americans often feel that nothing has been accomplished if they have not received some cognitive instruction.

A possible meeting schedule would have the group be called to order by its leader who begins the meeting with a prayer. After introduction of visitors, the brief sharing of news and announcements and a few songs, the leader gives a short (fifteen-to-twenty minute) message from the Bible.

This should be a strong effort to provide a Bible study of substance—one which focuses with intensity on a few passages of Scripture, so members will feel that they learned something new during this short study. Next, the group should include the sharing of concerns. Initially, these will deal primarily with "safe" concerns like illnesses and deaths in the family, but as trust develops and as the leader opens up more personal issues, members will feel free to talk about unsaved relatives and friends, inadequate prayer lives, job difficulties, and other personal problems. Too much time can easily be spent in this activity, so the leader must gently prod things along on some occasions.

Prayer follows the sharing of concerns. The leader designates one person to start, and then people pray for a few minutes each around the room as they see fit. The leader closes in prayer when everyone is finished. After prayer, there should be a time of informal fellowship. Coffee, tea, soda pop, and light snacks can be provided by the host. The meeting should end after a half an hour of fellowship. Generally, people will leave without prodding, but occasionally the leader will have to remind people of the need for sleep or to relieve baby-sitters.

Cell groups normally should be neighborhood based. In this way members do not have to drive long distances to their meetings and can respond more easily when support or crisis assistance is needed. To develop neighborhood groups, a church can divide its membership into zones using zip code maps and then assign families to neighborhoods groups within these zones. This implies, of course, that the entire membership will be assigned to a cell group. Some may feel that such an effort is starting out too large, but experience has shown that when a church begins with only those who are excited about the program, those who choose not to participate will become critics.

A special effort must be made to involve older persons in leadership roles so these powerful individuals will end up fighting for the program rather than against it. Efforts also should be made to insure that Sunday School is not seen as subordinate to the cell groups. The programs should receive similar emphasis and comparable organizational support. In most churches, this means that a home cell group director should be added as an office alongside the Sunday School director. A traditional church should not add staff to oversee the home cell program if a similar position does not exist already for Sunday School.

Where and when to meet can be major problems. We suggest rotating the meeting location among the five-to-seven-family units which make up each cell group (a few more if all are single). The groups will normally meet on a weeknight, although some downtown churches may consider substituting the groups for their Sunday evening worship service. We do not necessarily advocate this change, however. Wednesday night is also a possibility, but in most traditional churches the groups will meet on Monday, Tuesday, Thursday, or Friday. Of these, Friday evening may be the most popular.

As mentioned earlier, children sometimes can be very disruptive in cell group meetings and generally should not be allowed to attend the entire meeting until they are in their teens. One solution is to allow children to come in briefly at the beginning to sing songs, listen to a children's message and then retire to another room. Here a baby-sitter or group member could keep the young children occupied while the parents, single adults, and older children finish the cell group meeting.

Our final recommendation for traditional denominational churches is to design home cell groups to be growth oriented. Using the model of the Yoido Full Gospel Church, the cell groups should grow and multiply. Cell group pastors should identify and help train new leaders, and members should be encouraged to invite friends to the meetings.

Groups which are organized only for the benefit of their own members tend to become stagnant. They miss the joy of seeing men and women converted and coming to a closer relationship with Christ, and they stifle an organization which grows naturally. Cell group worship is attractive, and new people will attend if they are welcome. Even more so than the house church, the home cell group has unbounded growth potential. Few churches will ever grow to have fifty-thousand cell groups, but we know of no other strategy which allows even a fraction of such massive growth.

New Churches Through Home Cell Groups

One of the most effective ways of beginning home cell groups and new churches is to do so at the same time. This avoids the problems experienced by older churches which try to add home cell groups to an existing program of ministry. It would also seem to be a natural extension of a traditional church-planting technique.

Most new Southern Baptist churches begin through Bible studies in homes. In some cases a single Bible study may grow so large that it moves to a school or other rented facility and becomes a church, while in other cases several Bible studies organized by a church planter are merged to form a new congregation. We would suggest, however, that the Bible studies be allowed to *remain* as home cell groups after they have merged organizationally to form a new church. This is a strategy being used effectively in the San Francisco Bay area of California by Tony Rosenthal.

Rosenthal began his innovative approach to church planting while a student at Golden Gate Baptist Theological Seminary. He started with a Bible study in his home with a few neighbors who showed some interest. Eventually, this group grew large enough to divide, and one Bible study became two. In truth, the groups were more than Bible studies as they also included lengthy periods of prayer, fellowship, and sharing of needs. Because of their rapid expansion and the lack of leadership, Rosenthal led all the Bible study/cell groups in the beginning.

When potential leaders began to emerge, however, they were trained and took over several of the home groups.

From a cluster of neighborhood Bible studies, there emerged a new church. When the groups were strong enough, the participants decided that they were ready to become a church. Rented facilities were obtained, and the first services were held on a Sunday morning. Unlike most new church starts, this step did not mean the end of the Bible studies. They have continued and are very close in design to the home cell groups of the Yoido Full Gospel Church.

Another innovation developed by Rosenthal is to disband cell groups if they do not grow and divide within six months. His rationale is that the groups tend to become stagnant, inward looking, and complacent if the members are not actively seeking to win lost persons and invite them to their group. To avoid the tendency of close fellowship groups to form bonds so strong that new persons are not able to penetrate, the pastor disbands the group and disperses its members to other groups. This "threat" keeps the primary purpose of the groups clear to members.

The strategy of starting a new church through home cell groups and keeping the cell structure once the church is organized would seem to be particularly effective for a mainline denomination. As we have seen, most of the problems experienced by traditional churches have come from defenders of traditional institutions in the church who felt their program of ministry was being threatened. Rosenthal's strategy avoids this by essentially making the cell groups a traditional part of the new church. They actually precede the Sunday School in the organization of the church, and all founding members would have joined the church first through involvement in home worship. This is a procedure which has great potential and should be used widely.

Conclusions

Home worship is not new to Christianity in the United States. Throughout our history, Christians have met, prayed, and worshiped in their own homes and in the homes of friends. At the same time, mainline churches have grown larger on the average, and the intimate quality of worship that once existed in our churches often has been lost.

Changes also have occurred in the larger society which have made shallow relationships more pervasive and close ties less frequent. Many reactions to these changes can be observed in our society as people have sought meaning and intimate bonds in the most unlikely of places. Churches have not, by and large, responded to the need for community, but instead have stuck to their programs and worship schedules as if American society had remained static. Home worship is a grass-roots reaction to the changes in society and to the failure of mainline churches to act. In our view it is also a reaction to a functional deficiency in our churches which was only brought to light through the example of churches in the Third World.

The house church and the home cell group are innovations around which movements are forming. As with all movements, there are instability and some bad examples. This, however, should not keep denominational leaders in the United States from realizing the inherent functionality of home cell groups and house churches. They provide for fellowship, mutual support, caring, intense prayer, and the expression of Christian love in natural systematic ways. Few traditional churches can do so except in a haphazard fashion.

In this book we have tried to present an accurate description, analysis and evaluation of the many types of home-related worship found in the United States. Also, in this chapter we have tried to show how mainline churches and denominations can be involved. We began this study as objective observers but finished with the belief that the home cell group and the house church have a definite contribution to make to Christianity. If nothing else, they should make us aware that there are many ways and many settings in which we can worship God. Our structures and methods can be hindrances to the gospel, yet they should not be. Let us be open to new approaches which will help us fulfill the Great Commission.

Notes

1. Efforts have been made to start high-rise house churches in the United States and elsewhere. See "Evangelizing High-Rise Dwellers" by William Leslie in *Urban Review*, Apr. 1986, pp. 3-12.

2. The Indigenous Satellite Program has been successful in starting many new satellite congregations. The effort to divide and multiply congregations, however, has not been successful as yet. Satellites are started one by one through the efforts of the host church rather than through the planned division of house groups.

3. We refer to the "resource mobilization" approach to the origin of social movements. See Mancur Olsen, *The Logic of Collective Action* (New York: Schocken, 1968); and Mayer N. Zald and John McCarthy, *The Dynamics of Social Movements* (Cambridge, Mass.: Wintrop, 1979).